C.L.R. JAMES

PANTHEON BOOKS
60 YEARS OF PUBLISHING

C.L.R. JAMES

A LIFE

Farrukh Dhondy

PANTHEON BOOKS, NEW YORK

Pantheon Books and colophon are registered
trademarks of Random House, Inc.

Library of Congress Cataloging-in-Publication Data

Dhondy, Farrukh.
C.L.R. James: a life / Farrukh Dhondy.
p. cm.
ISBN 0-375-42100-9
1. James, C.L.R. (Cyril Lionel Robert), 1901-
2. Authors, Trinidadian—20th century—Biography.
3. Revolutionaries—Trinidad—Biography.
4. Intellectuals—Trinidad—Biography.
5. Historians—Trinidad—Biography. I. Title.

PR9272.9.J35 Z66 2002
813'.52—dc21 [B]   2001036519

www.pantheonbooks.com

Book design by Mia Risberg

Printed in the United States of America
First American Edition
2 4 6 8 9 7 5 3 1

CONTENTS

PROLOGUE

A university cricket match is in progress at a ground in Oxford in 1952. In the almost empty stands sits a tall black man in his fifties, wearing a floppy hat to shield him from the mild sun. He is watching the game intently. Across the field an undergraduate, a Caribbean of Indian origin, nudges the captain of Oxford, who is following his team's batting from beyond the boundary.

'Do you know what that negro is doing?' he asks.

'Having a day off?'

'No, he is reporting the match for the *Manchester Guardian*.'

The very notion gives rise to some hilarity. The Caribbean undergraduate picks up a reputation for being something of a wag. What he asserts, of course, is true. The lone black man in his fifties is C.L.R. James who writes cricket reports for the *Guardian* as an assistant to Neville Cardus and the young scholar who recognizes him comes from Trinidad, the Caribbean island colony from which James originates. He is V.S. Naipaul.

A black man writing cricket reports for a national newspaper was unusual in the 1950s. James had been recently deported from the United States and was back in England earning a modest living through journalism and pursuing besides his aim of world revolution; a lone man with a big dream. He had left the Caribbean twenty years before, convinced that his theatre of literary operation was the world at large and Britain in particular.

Thirty years after this cricket match, in the 1980s, C.L.R. James lived for a short period in my house in south London as guest and companion. He had passed his eightieth birthday and was in a very small way an intellectual celebrity in certain circles, primarily among students and followers of the resurgent 'black consciousness' that had materialized in the sixties and seventies as the Civil Rights movement in America and the movements for independence from European colonial rule in Africa. Students and researchers from the burgeoning black studies departments of American universities would drop in to the house with their tape recorders to talk to the sage.

They'd find 'Nello', a diminutive of his middle name, Lionel, surrounded by newspapers and books. He'd give them his time, scratching his full head of white hair and speaking in an accent he had retained from his youth, an accent more 'British' than today's singsongish and colourful Trinidadian, but crisp and colloquial.

One such researcher who was working on the Civil Rights movement, a young black man, arrived one afternoon. He was obviously in awe of James. He asked permission to switch on his tape recorder and C.L.R. nonchalantly waved his agreement. The young man's first question was itself a thesis. He began talking of Marxism as the philosophy of a 'white man'.

I was listening and knew that he had cast down a provocative gauntlet and looked forward to James's reply. James said nothing. He asked me for another toasted crumpet, referring to it, while making a circular motion of his right index finger against his outstretched left palm, as 'one more of those round things with holes', pretending, I thought, to have forgotten what they were called.

I fetched more toasted crumpets. When I returned the young man was telling C.L.R. that Marx was a Jew and a racist.

'Is that what he was?' asked C.L.R.

The sarcasm bounced like an arrow off Achilles.

'This is a remarkable insight, man,' C.L.R. added, addressing the crumpet which he now held in his hand.

The sarcasm was indeed lost on the researcher. He pressed on with questions about C.L.R.'s estimate of the Civil Rights movement's leaders. C.L.R. was fulsome about Martin Luther King and then suddenly stopped. He had lost interest in the interview. He had caught himself, probably for the umpteenth time, casting pearls before swine. I intervened and said it was Mr James's rest and TV time. The young man left.

'These fellers are not very bright are they?' he said.

I replied that perhaps we had treated him a trifle peremptorily.

'No man, these fellers . . . they go on about Marx and the Civil Rights movement. There is one thing I could have told him. The Civil Rights movement began with nylon.'

'With what?'

'This nylon. Tery . . . what is it called, the stuff they make sheets and shirts out of . . .'

'Terylene? What's that got to do with Martin Luther King?'

'That was what happened in the American South. These fellers invented artificial stuff which replaced cotton. They made it out of oil or some goddam thing in the laboratory. And they could make it cheap. The cotton economy was destroyed. The fellers who used to pick up a few dollars picking and sifting the cotton were thrown off the plantations.'

The old man was in full flow now. He was animated, acting the whole thing out.

'The Southern economy was destroyed and the workers and sharecroppers and all of them had to find some way out of that. Some way of going on, man. They followed the people who were offering them something. If it hadn't been Martin it would have been Harry. There was nothing else to do.'

'So nylon caused the black revolution?'

The old man broke into a contemptuous chuckle. 'I wouldn't go that far.'

On another occasion, again with a sense of mischief and in order to express his impatience with any piety about race, he told a researcher who was talking to him about slavery: 'That was all very sad, and I've shed all my tears over it, but I'll tell you the real significance of the slave trade: the Europeans had to build larger ships. It opened up the world.'

The black American researcher to whom he was speaking couldn't believe his ears.

'Ah beg y'pardon?' he said.

'That's what I said, man. Slavery caused the Europeans to build large ships so that they could take all those people from one side of the Atlantic to the other and bring all the goods back here.'

The researcher packed his tape recorder and left in haste. C.L.R. intended to disconcert him. He had spent a fair part of his life writing about Marxism, civilization, democracy, freedom, the large abstracts of twentieth-century discourse. He had written the first dramatic history of a slave revolt in the Caribbean. The intellectual position he had evolved started with the fact of slavery. He felt he had gone further. He was himself the great grandson of black slaves in the Caribbean and as such was a colonial whose only language was English and whose education and reading were British and European.

In the history of slavery and racial adjustment, colonial rule and withdrawal, the nineteenth century was the one in which slavery was abolished. A good part of the twentieth was spent in the conflicts between races that had been thrown together by slavery and colonial conquest. The United States of America spent the century coming to terms with the Negro question, establishing the rights and future of its black citizenry. African colonies such as Zimbabwe and South Africa are even now forging a settlement, bloody in its course, between its native and settler populations.

C.L.R. James was the only intellectual of the black diaspora unequivocally to espouse and embrace the intellectual, artistic and socio-political culture of Europe. He saw its development as the destiny not only of the blacks but of the world. The twentieth century produced in America apostles of Africanization and Black Muslim separatists; Africa produced 'African socialists' and tribal despots like Idi Amin. C.L.R. James, historian and philosopher, uniquely submerged racial awareness and distinction to democratic and egalitarian goals.

This perspective, to which he staunchly held, didn't originate in the Marxism he picked up at the age of thirty-two and after, though it was reinforced by it. He himself felt that it originated in the sympathies generated by his very early readings in English literature and through his lifelong involvement with the disciplines, culture and spirit of the game of cricket.

It may seem absurd, or at least far-fetched, to associate affection for a game with so large an ambition as delineating the directions of the history of our time. But James's origins and life as a colonial in early twentieth-century Trinidad led uniquely but precisely to such an association.

Though he fancied himself as a political activist and twice in his life ventured into active political agitation, C.L.R. James was primarily a writer. He is the only Marxist whose Marxism will continue to make sense in the twenty-first century, because it is untainted by anything that the world associates with the ideas and practice of Stalinism, the Soviet Union or of the academic Marxists of Europe and America, such as Althusser, Balibar and Marcuse who deserve the oblivion that has overtaken them.

C.L.R.'s Marxism came to maturity in the United States and resulted in the finest effort to provide a historical description of contemporary American society, its instincts, its inclinations and its culture. He has been called the American Bolshevik, but this is itself a misnomer and perhaps even an insult because one of the central tenets of this evolved Marxism is that the Bolshevik Party cannot serve as a model for American activity. That activity will arise from the frustrations and search for freedom of the American masses.

· · ·

C.L.R. James's work and life have never been subject to the critical scrutiny they deserve. A few dedicated US and Caribbean academics, specialists in black history, have written appreciations which seem to accept James as a founder and continuing influence on the rise of the black movement in the US and throughout the world. None of them has pointed out that in his own genesis, even in his writings and pronouncements, he was an unlikely godfather to this racially conscious radicalism. None has pointed out that he had nothing to do, either with gangs of 'revolutionaries' who claimed inspiration from him and murdered each other in the Caribbean, or with the black separatists and factions within the Black Muslim movement of the US who spoke of white people as the 'devil'.

C.L.R. James has had scant attention from serious commentators on history. E.P. Thompson, Marxist historian, author of *The Making of the English Working Class* (1963), in a TV conversation in 1984 remarked that the older C.L.R. James became, the more dangerous he got. The remark was well intentioned but begged the question as to why E.P. Thompson had never engaged with James's writings even though they were seminal arguments with Marxism, Thompson's pet subject.

If it had not been for the black movements of the sixties and seventies, the upheaval for rights and reforms in the United States and the institution of black studies in universities all round the world, the work of C.L.R. James would probably have disappeared without historical trace. It was through this movement and the restlessness and political agitation of the immigrants to Britain that I came across and subsequently met and befriended C.L.R. James. Having come to Britain as a student in 1964 and having stayed on, I sought the company of other immigrants and spent many years and a lot of energy in 'black' and Indian organizations. I did what Lenin said revolutionaries should do: I was loyal to my group; participated in discussion; wrote articles for publication; investigated phenomena; propagandized the hapless public; learned to speak where two or more had gathered together; demonstrated on the streets; was arrested on occasion; took part in strikes, and gave the better part of day and night to the 'cause'.

There were wild forces at play at the time. From some of these wild forces came an antipathy to everything 'Western', which included Marx. All Western culture was denounced as hypocrisy, giving rise to and tolerating slavery, and abolishing it only when it became unprofitable. Discovering C.L.R. James at this time, while I was interacting every day with this brand of anger and indirection, was like finding a port in a storm.

In these organizations, I was thrown together with West Indian 'exiles' and I found common ground with people from other former British colonies. The pink that spread over the map of the world, the reality and meaning of the Pax Britannica began in this camaraderie to make sense.

Even then, in the late sixties and seventies, this politically active group regarded themselves as exiles rather than as settlers in Britain. One of them was Darcus Howe, a Trinidadian and the grand nephew of C.L.R. James. I first met Darcus on a tube train when he tried to sell me a newspaper called the *Black Eagle*. It was not much of a paper, more of an agitational rag. My companions and I were on the way back from a demonstration against the Vietnam War, going home to our bedsits, when he accosted us. We bought a paper. He tried to sell us another copy.

One of us said, 'Thanks, comrade, we'll share it.'

'And you'll share the same jail sentence?' this black man asked. The question made rhetorical sense but it made us laugh and we began to talk.

Some months later, through the persuasion of an Indian student friend called Sunit Chopra, I joined one of these agitational groups, the Black Panther Movement, or BPM. It was not the same militant group that took to arms and street fighting in the USA, but was inspired by its experience and sought to recruit West Indian and Asian members to British black politics.

I met Darcus again when he brought C.L.R. James to speak to

the group in a house in Islington's then unfashionable Barnsbury. The house was owned by a young, rich, white woman who sympathized with the politics of the black movement and allowed, for a while, a commune of students and pamphleteers to live there.

The BPM had some weeks before mobilized itself to protest at the trial, at the Old Bailey in London, of four of its members. The defendants had taken part in a demonstration to protest against the constant police harassment of a black-owned restaurant called The Mangrove. This demonstration, attended by a few thousand, mostly young blacks, confronted a force of policemen on the streets of Notting Hill, west London, and the confrontation led to a small riot. Nine of those who were arrested in this affair were charged with riot, affray and, more seriously, with conspiracy to riot.

Four of these nine were members of the Black Panther Movement and it followed that the rest of the Movement dedicated its time and political energy to following the trial and building public opinion to combat their possible conviction. I was assigned the task of attending the trial and at the end of each day had to write up a summary of the proceedings in a partial way, pointing up the injustices of the British legal system and the innocence of my 'comrades'. These bulletins were then typed up and sent by post to several sympathetic left-wing groups and publications round the world.

James had been invited on a tour of inspection of our group and had been asked to speak about 'The Purpose of Organization'. I had never heard anyone like him. He was fluent, insightful, penetrative and immediate. He said nothing obvious, nothing patronizing. He knew to whom he was talking and brought all his erudition to bear.

C.L.R. had a more direct demeanour than most lecturers I had heard. When he spoke, he engaged with the small problems that his audience was grappling with and spread them on a larger canvas, giving them a history, significance and importance. He never spoke about a subject without assessing in a shrewd and instinctive way what his audience would want from him. In subsequent lectures and in later years I heard him do this again and again. He would penetrate the preoccupation of an audience having assessed them at a glance, and give their worries and wants deep historical depth. The defendants in a trial arising out of a small riot in Notting Hill would be made to feel like modern-day Dreyfuses. A slight novel by a black woman writer would be related very convincingly to some particular twist or advancement in sensibility brought about by Shakespeare or Dickens.

In the following years I was sporadically involved with C.L.R. James. We became friends. I drove him where he wanted to go, sometimes to lectures, sometimes to eat in restaurants we'd picked out in Soho and elsewhere. He would look for restaurants recommended to him forty years before and only after driving around for half an hour would he concede that they might have fallen victim to the years.

On one occasion I accompanied him to the studio of Anthony Armstrong-Jones who had been commissioned by the *Sunday Times* to provide portraits for their magazine feature. He had come to their attention as an eminence of the black British world. They had never featured him before. Armstrong-Jones and the reporter who came to interview James for the article that accompanied the photographs talked to him about cricket. They knew him as the cricket writer, even though they were aware of the fact that he was not being interviewed as the cricket writer and *aficionado* of the game but as a phenomenon in the black world.

This cover write-up in the *Sunday Times* triggered an urge in him to write his autobiography. He had covered his early years and his lifelong association with cricket in *Beyond a Boundary*. But there was another autobiography to write.

'I will put the whole thing down, man. You must take it down.'

I wasn't the only one to whom he began dictating his autobiography. His secretary and companion in the years after he left my house, Anna Grimshaw, says in her Foreword to her edited collection of C.L.R.'s letters that he attempted several times to dictate his autobiography to her. She says he couldn't piece it together. The difficulty was getting away from the formulation of *Beyond a Bound-*

ary. He now seemed to have no other way of looking at himself. Anna Grimshaw concludes that the letters must take the place of the autobiography.

Reading *Beyond a Boundary* one comes to the conclusion that C.L.R. never really wanted to write an autobiography. He wanted to present the world he grew up in and observe within it the development of the character he sees himself as. The letters Grimshaw edits get us no closer to the man. They are, as a subsequent chapter devoted to them contends, interesting theories on everything with no self-consciousness to go with them.

The attempts at the autobiography would be shelved in the very hour they were begun. He would tire of dictating and then ask me to refer my next question to the original book.

And yet everything he told me about his background during this process struck a chord. His political adventures and insights, though far removed from mine, remain for me a template of how to view and get under the surface of political situations and collective motives. His literary explorations, uneducated by the critical traditions of Oxford or Cambridge, are primitive and sophisticated at the same time. I wanted to write about C.L.R. because he openly acknowledges his debt to, and origins in, the colonizing culture, and then generates a defiance to its injustices using its own system of thought, history and logic.

Why read or write about another man's life unless it illuminates an aspect of yours?

C.L.R. JAMES

England Expects

> My chief memory is of my mother sitting reading and I lying on the floor near her reading until it was time to go to bed—9 o'clock. She was a very tall woman, my colour, with a superb carriage and so handsome that everybody always asked who she was. She dressed in the latest fashion—she had a passion for dress and was herself a finished seamstress. But she was a reader. She read everything that came her way. I can see her now, sitting very straight with the book held high, her *pince-nez* on her Caucasian nose, reading till long after midnight.[1]

This is probably C.L.R. James's earliest recorded memory. In fact, all we have of his childhood is what he tells us, for there are no witnesses to his birth and early childhood; C.L.R. outlived them all.

Cyril Lionel Robert James was born on 4 January 1901 in Tunapuna, Trinidad. His father, Robert, was a schoolteacher, the son of a sugar estate worker and his mother, Bessie, was one of three sisters, daughters of Joshua Rudder, a railroad fireman, originally from Barbados. Josh, as he was known, worked the single line from Port of Spain in the north to San Fernando in the south. The railroad carried wagon after wagon of sugarcane produce, the raw cane one way, the partially refined sugar the other.

Josh worked the line in more ways than one, having relationships with various women who lived on the railroad route. Bessie's mother was one of them, bearing not only Bessie, but two other girls, Florence and Lottie, before dying giving birth to Josh's next child. In late nineteenth-century Trinidad, fifty years after slavery was abolished, Josh knew that the girls would have been miserably treated by a stepmother. Instead, he sent the three girls to a Wesleyan convent, a school in the south of Trinidad where orphans or girls without mothers went. He entrusted them to the care of the nuns who would give them an education as well as turn them into eligible young ladies. Having left his daughters in safe hands, Joshua proceeded to make more than twenty-five other children up and down the railroad.

Bessie met Robert, C.L.R.'s father, at a function held by the church in the Trinidadian deep south, at a place called New Grant. James Sen. was the head of the school there, and responsible for a hundred or more rural children. He was there as part of a system by which novice schoolmasters in the employ of the Government had to do their stint in a country school before they could apply for a transfer to a city school.

Robert James met Bessie in the institution of the church and married her in it. The church dominated the lives of the emergent black professional class at the turn of the nineteenth century. Robert proposed formally to Bessie and their union was solemnized by the church. This was the procedure that Robert's employers, white British colonial administrators, would have approved. It wasn't the way his father-in-law Josh had chosen.

Robert and Bessie soon had two boys and then a girl: Eric, Cyril Lionel Robert and Olive.

New Grant was a place of sugar—acres and acres of cane with straight roads and smaller paths winding in and out of the plantations. Their population was mainly Indian, people on 'sub-indentures', which were contracts made in India with the labourers who had volunteered or been pressed into coming to the West Indies for a fixed term. Most of these indentured labourers had served their terms and decided to remain in Trinidad. They had, however, brought something of India with them. There was a temple and a mosque in the New Grant area. Christian converts went to church.

The James family was clearly differentiated from the cane cutters with whose children C.L.R. went to school. The cane cutters lived clustered around the farmlands, in clumps of houses near the road, along which bullock-drawn carts pulled loads of cut cane. The teacher's house, like that of the vicar and those of the railway employees, was different, and significant in the community. C.L.R. left no description of his childhood home, but John La Rose, Trinidadian poet and publisher who lived in the neighbourhood as a boy, speaks today of the James's house as one of the distinguished houses of the district, large and overlooking the Savannah.

The black schoolteacher, Robert James, serving his imperial civil servant's stint in the sticks with his convent educated, house-proud wife, his daughter and his two sons, would have been considered, on the social scale of the area, several notches above the peasantry who cut the cane and sent their children to his school. The family would have mixed with the English vicar of the local church and would have been considered almost on equal terms with the French Creoles in the area.

C.L.R., his friends and the children of the Indian labourers, all went to 'Mr James's school' as it was known locally. The school year lasted six months, being tied to the agriculture cycle of the sugar belt, and even then the sons of the labourers went to school only when they were not needed to plant and harvest. C.L.R. himself spent half the year with his grandmother and his two aunts in Tunapuna, thirty or so miles away.

Classes in the school were huge, a hundred pupils at a time. Robert James taught by rote and concentrated very hard on sifting out the brightest in the class, as it was to his advantage to gain as many scholarships to the urban schools as he could. He was paid in part by the results he obtained.

The Trinidad Government offered yearly free exhibitions from the elementary schools of the island to either of the two secondary schools, the Queen's Royal College and the Catholic College, St Mary's, both in Port of Spain. Today there are four hundred exhibitions but in those days there were only four. Through this narrow gate boys, poor but bright, could get a secondary education and in the end a Cambridge Senior Certificate, a useful passport to a good job.

There were even more glittering prizes to be won. Every year the two schools competed for three island scholarships worth £600 each. With one of these a boy could go abroad to study law or medicine and return to the island with a profession and independence. There were at that time few other roads to independence for a black man who started without means. The higher posts in the Government, in engineering and the scientific professions, were monopolized by white people, and, as practically all big business was also in their hands, coloured people were as a rule limited to the lower posts. Thus law and medicine were the only ways out.

Although ultimately C.L.R. didn't take either of these ways out, he did step on to the first rung of the ladder. He won an exhibition to Queen's Royal College at his second attempt in 1910, at the age of nine.

His father had first entered him for the exam when he was eight. Since students were able to sit this up to the age of eleven, James Sen. argued that this would give him four shots at it; in fact, he only needed two.

In his own words, C.L.R. was a country bumpkin, taken by his father to compete with the other ninety-nine boys sitting the exam. On the day itself, he says he watched the other 'fighting cocks' and their trainers who had gathered in the school hall to take the exam. He came seventh that first time. The next year, he stood first.

Looking back on his childhood from his eighties, James claimed to have been conscious of bringing himself up as a young English intellectual and confessed a certain precociousness which is borne out by his early success at the scholarship.

As always with C.L.R., it is his memories of his reading, and his introduction to the literature which was to become so important to him, which tell us most about his early education. He wrote, for instance, of the time he was inspired by a book called *The Throne of the House of David,* which contained abridged Bible stories. He went back to the original, much to the delight of his mother and his aunt Judith who watched the young man poring over the Bible not for the instruction but for stories to connect with the preaching he had heard in church. As he read, he noted the names of the books and the numbers of the chapters. And yet, at school he was still being given 'readers' with pedagogic prose, which he parodied as 'Johnny's father had a gun and went shooting in the forest'.

It was his mother who inspired his reading. She read voraciously herself and passed on her books to him. The only fact James conveys about her is that she was a tireless reader—of novels, any novels; Scott, Thackeray, Dickens, Hall Caine, Stevenson, Mrs Henry Wood, Charlotte Brontë, Charlotte Braeme, Balzac, Hawthorne. It was also his mother who introduced him to Shakespeare and he remembered in particular her edition, in which each play was fronted with an illustration with the act and scene reference below it. This stayed with him throughout his life, as did all his reading, as he would insist whenever talking autobiographically:

> Now I could not read a play of Shakespeare but I remember perfectly looking up the Act and Scenes stated at the foot of the illustration and reading that particular scene. I am quite sure that before I was seven I had read all those scenes. I read neither before nor after, but if the picture told me Act 3, Scene 4, I would look it up and fortified myself with the picture.

Any middle-class child who grew up in the early twentieth century in the English-speaking world will recognize that illustrated Shakespeare. There was also the definitive Dickens or, for colonials from the Indian subcontinent, FitzGerald's *Rubaiyat of Omar Khayyam,* an *Arabian Nights* or a volume of Kipling's stories. They were there on the family bookshelf, or if one came from more literate stock, bookshelves. The memory has the ring of remembered truth.

Other reading informed James's early education. There were, for example, the magazines that were brought to the door of the James's house in New Grant by an itinerant bookseller—*The Review of Reviews, Tit-Bits, Comic Cuts, The Strand Magazine, Pearson's Magazine*, 'sixpenny copies of the classics'.

The book which C.L.R. first read at the age of eight, though, and to which he returned throughout his life, was *Vanity Fair*. He claimed in later years to have read it on average once every three months. In his eighties he was still reading it and he would, with mischievous delight, ask one to read aloud from it and himself finish the paragraph after listening to its first sentence. Not perfectly, but well enough, paraphrasing the content if he wasn't able to reproduce it verbatim. He wrote about the book and talked about it and about other works by Thackeray, but never used him as he used Shakespeare, and later Melville, to construct extended critical and political theories. Shakespeare became for him an instrument of history; Melville the essence of his political understanding of America. Thackeray was not treated in the same way. Thackeray and *Vanity Fair* remained personal, unanalysable, a childhood memory and then a lifelong pursuit.

Why it was his particular favourite was never clear. All he would say, in later life, was that he owed more intellectually to Thackeray than he did to Marx. His political ideas had grown to embrace literature in a particular way by the time he was fifty, but that boy of eight who read *Vanity Fair* must have taken away something more lasting, more connected with the observed world, something that C.L.R. hardly ever articulated.

In this first chapter of C.L.R.'s life, it was partly literature which differentiated him and his family from the boys with whom he went to school. He is the boy with the books, with the mother who reads by the hearth, sitting on a rocking chair by a lamp. The boy sits on the rug within its circle of light, on the wooden floor, leafing through the illustrations in the *Collected Shakespeare* or some other book which testifies to their gentility and distance from the cane workers.

Winning the island scholarship to Queen's Royal College began a new stage in C.L.R.'s life. It brought him for the whole year, with the exception of the holidays, to the town. He lived in his grandmother's house in Tunapuna, Port of Spain, and this thrust him into his first real contact with the semi-urban black population of professionals, workers, men who lived by their wits and men and women who fell beyond the repair of wit into the abyss.

One of the characters that James met in Tunapuna, and later wrote about in *Beyond a Boundary,* was called Matthew Bondman. The Bondmans were neighbours of his grandmother and aunts, who had no time for any of the family, with the exception of the father. They 'detested' Matthew, whom they saw as a scowling ne'er-do-well who shamelessly walked barefoot up the main street; they considered his sister Marie nothing but a slut.

C.L.R.'s description of him in *Beyond a Boundary* shows us why his polite bourgeois family might have felt this way:

> He was a young man already when I first remember him, medium height and size, and an awful character. He was generally dirty. He would not work. His eyes were fierce, his language was violent and his voice was loud. His lips curled back naturally and he intensified it by an almost perpetual snarl.[2]

We can imagine the young James being fascinated by this character, as he looked into the abyss from which a precarious gentility, with its manners, its habits of work and speech and its universal reading—more than anything else its reading—had preserved him.

But for James, Matthew had a skill that went beyond even this—he could bat. He was fascinated with the man's batting skills, his grace, his style and his energy, and this already meant a great deal to him.

The Bondman description is important for another reason, however. In it we see the first awakenings of James the writer. In these recollections of early childhood we see him observing characters, capturing the half-heard whispers of scandal and the hints of depravity in the circumlocution of the aunts which he knew 'had something to do with "men" '. We see the beginnings of the inclusive sympathy that a novelist or historian must cultivate for his characters, and the beginning of his ability to assess exactly the positions of people in the society into which he had been born.

Queen's Royal College, still Trinidad's proudest school, was run at the time by Oxbridge graduates, all public school men, stamped with the Arnoldian ethos. It was the great period of consolidated empire, the later Victorian and early Edwardian era, from the last decades of the nineteenth century to the first of the twentieth. The Boer War had ended in a draw with new lessons of brutality learnt. The Indian National Movement had only just begun and the demand for Indian independence had not yet resulted in mass agitation. Curzon had held his imperial Durbar, the high point of British suzerainty for those territories of the world map that were coloured pink. The First World War was not yet foreshadowed.

Who were these men who chose to go out not as colonial administrators or soldiers, doctors and businessmen, the boxwallahs of empire, but as teachers? They were young men without a priestly vocation, rebels against the strict conventions of the colonial law makers and administrators, liberal in the sense that they worked dedicatedly to educate a colonial, coloured and black middle class, and trained it to take on some of the responsibility of running the empire.

These men who came out from England brought with them no patronization of 'natives'. The boys were the boys. They would be schooled in maths and Latin, French, Greek, English grammar and English history, in the Bible and Shakespeare, as rigorously as lads at Rugby or Eton. In addition they would be taught cricket and made to 'play the game', to live by the system of ethics for which James uses the rules and spirit of cricket as a metaphor.

C.L.R. never remembered any individual teacher of his with any vividness although he mentioned the Principal of the college, Mr W. Burslem, whom he called 'part Pickwick and part Samuel Johnson'. Mr Burslem was kind to him and invited him, as a mark of favour, to do small personal tasks for him.

It was also, however, Burslem who reported him to the Board of Education as a failing pupil when James fell behind in his studies, and withdrawal of his exhibition was threatened. Boys who had won exhibitions and were being paid for out of the public purse were expected to devote a lot of energy to their studies, to excel in them and eventually to win island scholarships to British universities, ending up perhaps as native members of the island's Legislative Council. To Burslem and to James's parents, the young C.L.R. was a disappointment. His two passions were not taking him down the road towards the island scholarship. He was absorbed in his self-imposed programme of reading the school and town libraries dry. And he was obsessed with cricket.

The complaint to the Board was a blow to the prestige of the James family as the event was recorded and reported in Board minutes and thence in the newspapers. The Jameses were teachers by profession. C.L.R.'s godfathers were teachers; the family's most respected friends were teachers; it was ignominious for the young C.L.R. to be threatened with the withdrawal of his exhibition.

James later told me that serious family matters were settled by family conferences, which seems to mean that the women of the household also had a voice in the decisions. Such a conference was called and it was decided to impose restrictions on the boy. He was to catch the first train home after the bell went for the end of the school day, and to play no cricket at all.

But C.L.R. couldn't stick to this discipline. He would be on the cricket field after school and he invented duties that the masters had allocated to him on Saturdays. He lied and cheated and borrowed clothes, bicycles, money, anything that was necessary to dodge the imposed disciplines and curfews and escape to the cricket grounds. Then the entire fabric of deceit collapsed and the forgeries and borrowings, the debts and lies all came to light. His father beat him. Corporal punishment was a routine form of discipline at school and at home. By his own account, James was flogged.

By the account of one of the descendants of the family, the family story was that the beatings from his father stopped when C.L.R. was over fifteen years old and a strong, tall lad who told his father that, if the beatings continued, he would return the compliment. The rod was withdrawn.

At QRC, he began to collect facts about cricket, statistical analyses and the lives and the games of W. G. Grace and Ranjitsinhji. And together with the facts and the reading of cricket stories was the game itself, widely played at his school, supervised by the teachers and enthused with the spirit of fair play.

The game began to be an obsession. It was everywhere around him and the *Zeitgeist* of the time dictated that a man's quality was demonstrated by his abilities at cricket, his style by the flourish of his bat, his strength and stamina by his bowling and the speed of his reflexes by his fielding.

James's classmates with whom he shared the passion were for the large part children of white officials, white business men, middle-class blacks and mulattos, Chinese boys, some of whose parents still spoke broken English and one or two Indian boys whose parents could speak no English at all.

It was on this 'motley crew', as James calls it, that the ethic of cricket as the embodiment of team spirit, loyalty, endeavour, fair play, generosity in victory and forbearance in defeat was imposed.

Later, James admitted to early conflicts that arose between this ethic of 'fair play' and a more 'political' one. He found a name for the earlier one: 'Before very long I acquired a discipline for which the only name is Puritan.'[3]

Here, in his own words, is how he felt this ethical framework, acquired in that colonial school, translated into action:

I never cheated, I never appealed for a decision unless I thought the batsman was out, I never argued with the umpire, I never jeered at a defeated opponent, I never gave to a friend a vote or a place which by any stretch of imagination could be seen as belonging to an enemy or to a stranger. My defeats and disappointments I took as stoically as I could. If I caught myself complaining or making excuses I pulled up. If afterwards I remembered doing it I took an inward decision to try not to do it again. From the eight years of school life this code became the moral framework of my existence. It has never left me.

When C.L.R. James wrote those words in 1963, he was recalling feelings of fifty years before. By then, the decade before the rise of Black Power, a deadly fight for civil liberty in America, was already underway. A lot had happened to James since those schooldays. It is ironic that the man who admits to being intellectually shaped by a code that comes straight out of Rudyard Kipling's *If* should have become the hero of the generations who thought they were forging a new political ethic in the 1960s and seventies. The mood amongst them was anti-colonial, anti-puritan and severely satirical about any Kiplingesque values.

The Kiplingesque description of the fair play ethic, the cricketing metaphors in which it is enshrined, the sincerity with which the belief is held and the self-consciousness with which it is declared, do not square with the notions of a Marxist thinker, a Leninist executor or a black militant. Cricket ethics are, in the public imagination, identical with the moral system of the public schools that gave the sport its social organization. They are assumed to be synonymous with the rulers, not the rebels. And yet James bought the ethic of the public school and professed it as his own in almost religious terms: 'The Gospel according to St Matthew, Matthew being the son of Thomas, otherwise called Arnold of Rugby.'[4]

This was James at sixty-three acknowledging his debt to Dr Thomas Arnold, not only as the father of the poet and the founder of Rugby School, but as a symbol of the puritan ethic of Victorian Britain: the Bible, the Classics, cricket with its craft and morals.

This was, of course, an upbringing it was fashionable to deny, as he himself recognized in a story he told about a meeting in Manchester in 1956. Aneurin Bevin was replying to criticisms of 'not playing with the team' by satirically playing with the concepts of 'stiff upper lip' and 'playing with a straight bat'. The audience loved it, but C.L.R. was conscious that he 'was not going all the way' with Mr Bevan. And when Michael Foot, the other platform speaker, smiled, when introduced as 'an old public school boy', C.L.R. saw it as a 'cryptic' smile which showed that he too had his doubts.

Bevin, at some point during the speech, said, 'I did not *join* the Labour Party, I was brought up in it.' In his recollection of the speech, James added, 'And I had been brought up in the public school code.'

James called his school 'our little Eden'. The inevitable fall, a relatively insignificant one, came in 1918 when James was about to finish school.

The First World War was still being fought in Europe and men had left the island as recruits to the empire war effort. The 'public contingent' was recruited by the Government of the island from the working classes and the peasants. The 'Merchants' Contingent' consisted of the young men of the upper classes, the worthies of the society, whose white and mulatto sons went straight to England to join English regiments.

James recalled that one morning when he should have been at school he presented himself at the 'Merchants' Recruiting Office' and offered himself as officer material. The recruiting office was doing a brisk trade that day. One young man after another went in and was interviewed. They were asked for references and were sent for further physical and aptitude tests. Then came James's turn. The interviewing 'Merchant' took one look at the black-skinned boy before him and motioned him away rudely. It was what James had been half expecting and it was his first conscious public challenge to the racist policy that had imported to the island with this process of recruitment to a European war. James was too polite to make a disruptive protest. He told the recruiting sergeant that he was perfectly qualified for recruitment and said he would take the matter further.

But with whom was he to take the matter further? James told the English sergeant of his school cadet corps of his experience and the man was indignant and angry. White boys from the school went away to be trained and came back, proudly wearing their uniforms before being shipped to the killing fields of Europe.

There is no evidence that C.L.R. terribly missed taking part in the First World War. In fact, he spoke of it only as the beginning of a new barbarism in Europe, taking millions of young lives in a destructive orgy unparalleled in history. In speeches he time and again used the statistics of death in combat and of the Holocaust to demonstrate how the civilized world in the twentieth century went repeatedly down the path of barbarism, into the cesspool of racial and nationalistic murder.

The irony was that James, who had been reading the work of Wilfred Owen and Siegfried Sassoon, made no connection between the public school ethic which he embraced and the slaughter of the trenches.

James's omission of the Great War in his own writings could be attacked in the way that the more hackneyed literary critic might criticize Jane Austen for never dwelling on the Napoleonic Wars. The difference is, of course, that Jane Austen did not go on to write political speeches denouncing the militarism of the Napoleons of her time. James did.

Another outstanding omission in his writing of the time was the Russian Revolution in 1917, the ten days that shook the world and created a new world order. James was to analyse and criticize this event in book after book in the thirties, forties, fifties and after. But at the time? He appeared to be oblivious, even though, according to Alfred Mendes, James's literary collaborator in the late twenties, the Revolution was widely reported. His Old World order continued without disturbance and he seems not to have become conscious of its importance until after he left school and, between 1919 and 1924, came into contact with people who had a wider vision of politics and contemporary history.

At the time, James tells us, he was content to follow his two obsessions: playing cricket and reading. He remembered reading everything he could about the history of cricket, and reading a set of Thomas Hardy's novels in the sequence in which they were published. This demonstrates an appetite for reading, but it also shows that James was reading without the benefit of any contact with critical minds or critical writing which would organize his reading for him. He wasn't reading because he had acquired any scheme of merit or critical differentiation between one book and another or even one novelist and another. The chronological order of publication was his only scheme.

This wasn't, of course, the only reading that James was doing during these years at Queen's College. In stark contrast to the tastes, skills and ambitions that his reading was inculcating in the young James were the sordid little publications with dirty pictures that his classmates would hand around.

Sex was not confined to reading. James noted in an unpublished manuscript referred to by Paul Buhle that from the ages of eleven to sixteen he masturbated, without the need for any fantasy objects and that he 'experimented with [his] bodily maturity' for pure physical pleasure. Then, at sixteen he seduced or was seduced by a schoolgirl of the same age. Whether through some sense of guilt or shame, or some inability to own up to sexual exploits in his puritan middleclass household we don't know, but we do know that he treated the whole experience of sex with the same intellectual seriousness that he treated everything else. He did what he always did when contemplating his entrance into experience; he read about it. So he read six volumes of *The Psychology of Sex* by Havelock Ellis at the age of sixteen, volumes he probably had to hide from his family.

James had not turned out to be the academic prodigy that had been expected when he won his exhibition. He wasn't an island scholar and he wasn't earmarked any more for the Legislative Council. But he had passed his exams, if indifferently. He graduated from school and was accepted back as a teacher by his school. James returned therefore to the Gothic stone and brick buildings of QRC adjoining the Savannah, to teach history.

Surprisingly, considering his later preoccupations, he had at this point no particular theory of history, no axe to grind. He taught the curriculum. But somewhere in the literary subconscious, theories of history were brewing. In an interview with Richard Small in the 1970s James recalled reading history books voraciously in this period. He remembered reading *A History of England* by Hilaire Belloc and the biography of Dickens by G. K. Chesterton. What was important about these was that they violently attacked the traditional English history on which he had been brought up and gave him a critical conception of historical writing.

But at the time James never made anything of this new theory of history. There he was, a black man teaching history in a pseudo public school in a crown colony in the 1920s. The curriculum he taught represented to him nothing more than the discipline necessary to turn out the next generation of members of the Legislative Assembly or the next generation of rebels with a cricketing cause.

The teaching of history in colonial schools in the century of decolonization posed a dilemma in the minds of many teachers. Like other 'native' teachers of history who, in small but increasing numbers, were replacing the British expatriate teachers in colonial schools, James had to teach history from books which justified Britain's colonial mission. By their nature these books glossed over the cruelties that the conquest of Africa and India and the settlement of the Caribbean islands had entailed.

How could the 'native' teacher handling and transmitting these texts not have had a sense of unease? One would expect that a teacher in James's position would have secretly rebelled against the entire project and adopted, clandestinely at least, the incipient nationalism that was coming to the surface in all colonial societies. James, however, displayed no such unease. When I asked him, in his eighties, how he had incorporated this paradox, he simply said: 'I wasn't thinking about that. My job was to teach those books and that history as the British wrote it and that's what I did.'

Decades later in my own school in India, ten or twelve years after Indian independence, when Nehru was Prime Minister, Bishop's School, Poona, was very much like Queen's Royal College, Trinidad, in its aims and its curriculum. I was taught by a few white teachers who stayed behind after the Raj. The rest were almost all Anglo-Indians, the term we used for people of mixed Indian and English blood.

Until I was twelve I was taught essentially as C.L.R. was in Trinidad, fifty years before, about Henry VIII and the destruction of the monasteries, about the Norman invasion, about the Black Hole of Calcutta and the generalship of Clive of India. When I was thirteen there came to our school a fiery and very black-skinned history teacher called Satya Martin. With his Indian first name and European surname, he was difficult to place precisely. We, the boys of the ninth standard, accepted him as our begowned new history teacher, but we knew from the first that behind those keen eyes there burned the zest of subversion.

I cannot say what devil moved him, but he was an Indian nationalist and a logical positivist to boot. He got us to throw away our history books and brought the lessons to life. He had a mission to subvert and to turn us, his teenage pupils, into nationalists. The British had exploited India. History did have villains, and they were white men. The browns were heroes except when they gave way to rank superstition in which he included all non-Christian religions.

At first the budding intellectuals of the ninth standard were suspicious of Mr Martin. There were his negative traits of which we didn't approve. He was too much of a 'gaspot', a braggart, unforgivable in our code. But we suspected that the headmaster didn't quite know what Mr Martin was peddling in his lessons, and we were not about to be the ones to betray him. What he was peddling was probably contraband history and, because it was smuggled intellectual property, we supported it.

James was in no way a Satya Martin. His denial of any radical purpose in these teaching years was categorical. He was getting his pupils to pass exams and the flame of revolt had not yet been lit in his consciousness.

James acknowledged no single radical influence that transformed him from the conventional, conservative history teacher, to the advocate of West Indian independence. None of his teachers was radical, though the remarks he attributes to his two headmasters may be seen as evidence of a liberal tendency.

It was when he was in his twenties, from 1921 to 1931, that James made the transition from being the non-radical history teacher, the apostle of puritanism, to the radical who believed in West Indian self-government. It was in these years that the idea that West Indians should and could govern themselves took hold.

And cricket had no small part to play in this conviction. Cricket had become a measure in his mind of excellence and of organization. Everywhere he looked West Indian society manifested this ability to organize and train and to be governed by the ethical spirit of the game.

C.L.R. implied that all the players in his Trinidad were animated by this spirit. When he talked of his attitude to cricket he used the pronoun 'we'. And not only the lads of Queen's Royal College played cricket. The whole society did. Cricket may have suffered from the segregation, racially and class-based, of teams but it was still, paradoxically, a cohesive force in that society. It brought interests and teams throughout society together. In that universality lay the reason for its becoming the second great disciplining and formative influence on James's life.

Cricket was the great even playing field. The West Indies in the early part of the twentieth century was inhabited by not only whites, mulattos of all shades and blacks, but by Chinese and Indian indentured labour, Portuguese people whose status as whites was assured but flavoured, and immigrant workers from other smaller islands. There was an intellectual elite, white, mulatto and black promoted through public education and all sorts of other castes and classes and divisions. The race question was, superficially at least, what it has always been, the question of the ratio of advancement to colour.

It is perhaps not surprising that it was in the arena of cricket that James's first real racial trial or dilemma arose.

After a year of cricketing glory with a second-class club, in which he established himself as a first-rate player, it was clear that he should play for one of the first-class clubs. It was the question of which club to join that caused a 'social and moral crisis which had a profound effect on [his] whole future life'.

The problem was that the various first-class cricket clubs reflected in detail the divisions of Trinidadian society. The Queen's Park Club was mostly for the white and wealthy, the only exceptions being a few coloured men from old established mulatto families. The Shamrock Club was Catholic and also almost exclusively white. You had to be a policeman to join 'Constabulary,' and 'Stingo' was the club of 'plebeians'—'totally black and no social status whatever . . .'

The choice was therefore between the two remaining clubs—Maple and Shannon. Maple was the club of the brown-skinned middle class. Colour was more important to them than class, so 'a lawyer or a doctor with a distinctly dark skin would have been blackballed, though light-skinned department-store clerks of uncertain income and still more uncertain lineage were admitted as a matter of course'. Shannon, on the other hand, was the club of the black lower middle class.

In talking of Shamrock, James noted with some glee that the children of a non-white had gained admittance through being Roman Catholic and owing to the fact that their father had been appointed Attorney-General to help quell a riot of commoners. A strategy of colonial pacification had therefore led to his advancement and subsequently to the breaking of the colour bar in a cricket club.

James's dilemma, he said, began to make him the subject of public controversy. There was even speculation in the press as to which club he would join. Even allowing for exaggeration, this presents us with the parochial scope of the Trinidadian press, absorbed, to whatever degree, with which club a junior player would join. A small place with small concerns. Elsewhere the Russian Revolution progressed.

James asked the advice of an old friend, himself a brown man, but 'one openly contemptuous of these colour lines'. The friend's advice was unequivocal: 'I understand exactly how you feel about all this God-damned nonsense. But many of the Maple boys are your friends and mine. These are the people whom you are going to meet in life. Join them; it will be better in the end.'

The one thing James didn't tell us was why he, a dark man, was acceptable to Maple with their colour-conscious policy. Perhaps it was because he was a teacher and was known as a cultivated man.

He joined Maple and played for them and agonized over what onlookers would make of him, a dark man keeping company with lighter-complexioned people, because for the negro 'the surest sign of . . . having arrived is the fact that he keeps company with people lighter in complexion than himself', as he later said.

Cricket was, as we have seen, from an early age a distraction from study and had already led to James not doing as well as he was expected to do in school. In later years, though, James admitted that this didn't give him anywhere near the 'inner stress' which was caused him by possibly being an arriviste who crossed one of the colour bars.

Why did he join Maple? Because it sounded plausible to him that he would spend his social or professional life with the lighter-skinned men of Maple? Because he wanted in some subconscious way to belong to a light-skinned club? Because his ambitions would be more easily advanced through their connections?

This is possible, but C.L.R. was clear that his only ambition at that time was to be a writer, even though he knew that that was an uncertain occupation, especially for a young man born in the West Indies which had produced no writers of note. The men of Maple are unlikely to have been able to assist him in this ambition.

· · ·

If C.L.R. seemed oblivious of the Russian Revolution, he also seems to have ignored the political events taking place much closer to home, in Trinidad itself. In 1919, Trinidad was going through turmoil. The longshoremen struck and closed down Port of Spain. The authorities were worried and called in troops from Jamaica, a thousand miles away. New laws were passed, giving powers of arrest and curfew and curtailing the freedom of association.

The strikes and some of the agitation were led by Captain Arthur A. Cipriani. He was a horse breeder and trainer of Corsican descent who had raised a regiment of black men in the First World War and had come back, with a bitter experience of racism in the British army and of trench warfare, to lead the Trinidad Workingmen's Association. If one ignores comparisons of scale, there is a parallel to Gandhi, who had been trained as a Middle Temple lawyer in London, went on to practise in South Africa and returned to India as a celebrity, a man with a reputation for opposition to British rule. He joined the Indian National Congress and transformed it from an organization of intellectuals into an instrument of mass revolt.

In the same way, Cipriani transformed the Trinidadian Workingmen's Association, formed in 1897 as an organization of businessmen who supported the claims and causes of labour, into a union of working men who would agitate for economic and political advance.

Like Gandhi, Cipriani was a natural leader. In 1922 he founded a magazine called *The Socialist* and began campaigning for better wages, for a reduction in working hours, for universal education and for the abolition of child labour. In 1926, Cipriani was elected Mayor of Port of Spain. He was a local hero.

By his own account, however, James only met Cipriani when he was researching and writing a history of revolt in the islands and sought an interview. He intended to build this history around the life of Captain Cipriani. The interview was granted and James wrote the book. It was one of the manuscripts he carried with him in 1932 to England.

James said later that Cipriani invited him to write on cricket and on history for *The Socialist*. Once or twice, he said he took the rostrum to speak in support of Cipriani's various candidates for elections to the Trinidad Assembly, although this could easily, as he was a civil servant, have cost him his job. There is, however, no evidence to corroborate the boast that James appeared on any platform for Cipriani. There are no articles by James in *The Socialist*, which means either that James didn't take up the invitation to write for it or that Cipriani didn't publish what he wrote. Cipriani did not ask him to join his organization or associate with the movement in any closer way.

The politics of the islands did not impinge on James in such a way as to cause him to change any aspect of his life or interests. He had no memory, neither is there any evidence, of his practical involvement in the island's political turmoil at that time.

We know about James's choice of cricket club and about his immersion in literature. This was the route the schoolmaster took to politics.

In 1919, as Cipriani was agitating for reform, James and several of his friends in Port of Spain founded the Maverick Club. The group included the writers Alfred Mendes and Albert Gomes, both Trinidadian Creoles of Portuguese origin.

The exact nature of the Maverick Club is not clear. On the one hand, it is portrayed as an exclusive black club by Richard Small in an essay entitled 'The training of an intellectual, the making of a Marxist'.[5] On the other hand, in *Beyond a Boundary*, C.L.R. himself says that it was a 'circle of friends, most of them white with whom we exchanged ideas, books, records and manuscripts . . . We lived according to the tenets of Matthew Arnold, spreading sweetness and light and the best that has been thought of and said in the world.'

Small has obviously got it wrong and wilfully so. He says the group was black and interposes a question—'what racial consciousness does this represent?'. The answer is 'none, because according

to James the group was white'. A black society giving cultural sem-
inars to whites seems novel and revolutionary to Richard Small but,
alas, it did not exist—or at least it was not the Maverick Club.

In Paul Buhle's biography of James, *C.L.R. James: The Artist As
Revolutionary,* published by Verso in 1988, the origin of the club is
viewed differently. Buhle writes:

> James' literary bent, meanwhile, began to impel him toward
> a cultural politics congruent with Cipriani's radical re-
> formism. James and his friends had thus formed the Maver-
> ick Club in 1919, for non-whites only, with James naturally
> as secretary—almost as if he had moved his cricket func-
> tions to another quarter. They published lectures, gave lec-
> tures and wrote essays on the usual subjects of English
> literature and drama.

Not only does Buhle also ignore the existence of a circle of white
friends mentioned by James but he gives the black group a character which is 'congruent with Cipriani's radical reform'. But in what
sense was it congruent? Was the club giving lectures on Wordsworth and English drama or wasn't it? And in what sense did leading an agitation for a minimum wage, Cipriani's activity, assume a
congruence with these cultural discussions among white, black and
mixed race friends?

The elision between James's literary doings and the radical politics in which he took no part may be wishful thinking by Buhle.
James's presence in a black-only group is the handle that Buhle
grasps to make this spreading of 'sweetness and light' 'congruent'
with Cipriani's agitational actions. The purpose, no doubt, was to
promote James as a race radical. This would be in keeping with the
1960s fashion for racially exclusive black political groups which
spread from America to Britain and for which white 'activists', far
from being disconcerted or bitter at their exclusion, expressed their
complete support.

With Mendes, C.L.R. brought out a magazine called *Trinidad,* whose first edition appeared at Christmas 1929. After two issues, the magazine folded and was subsumed in March 1931 into *The Beacon,* edited by Albert Gomes.

By Gomes's own account in his autobiographical sketch which precedes his novel *Black Fauns,* he was in the USA when James and Mendes brought out *Trinidad.* He considered it radical and accomplished, and it indicated to him that there was in his native island a stirring of literary activity and talent. It inspired him to return to Trinidad to join Mendes and James.

Mendes's account of how the magazine came about is enlightening. According to him, James confided in him that he wanted money in order to get married. Mendes suggested that they both do what they were best at, and that was to write. From that financial necessity came the idea of a magazine.

So, it was in fact with this circle of white friends, Gomes and Mendes included, that James began to write the first 'black literature' of the islands.

2

The Colonial
Prepares

Still in his twenties, James developed a radical literacy conviction. With Mendes, he began to write and publish in *Trinidad* and *The Beacon* stories which were set in the 'barrack-yard', the compounds where the poor urban strays of the black population lived. These 'barrack-yard' stories and later the barrack-yard novels, including James's *Minty Alley,* were the early blooms of the Caribbean's literary flowering.

James felt that he had discovered the material of his fiction and, as for so many writers, the subject matter presented itself. From experience and observation, with or without conscious thought, it arrives, like e-mail from the subconscious. In later life he was to tell me that he was convinced that the stories he could construct from his observations of the slums of Trinidad could stand side by side on the shelves with *Vanity Fair* and the novels of Thomas Hardy.

Before these stories could be written, such a conceit or conviction had to be fully formed, or else modesty and the fear of ridicule would have stifled the impulse to write. Secondly, some undergrowth had to be cleared, some weeds poisoned.

James encountered the weeds. Colonial literature existed, but to someone like James it was patronizing, even denigratory. Someone had to reply to it, out of indignation, or simply out of wanting to put the record straight. This point/counterpoint is part of the history of all colonies. It is perhaps the colonial's destiny to discover himself or herself first in critical prose, to see his or her reflection in a brutally truthful or a distorting mirror. The spell that pulls us into the mystery of written reality is the curse that damns us too.

In Poona, where I grew up in the fifties and early sixties, there was the Poona Philosophical Society, attended in the twenties and thirties by the teachers of philosophy and related disciplines at the university and by dilettantes, mostly white, who fancied themselves an intellectual cut above the rest. The white settlement in Poona in those days consisted of a heavy army garrison, a military hospital which served the whole of the south of India, and a civil administration for the regional 'Presidency' during the summer and monsoon months when Bombay, 120 miles away, became humid, hot and intolerable.

By the time I was introduced to the Poona Philosophical Society, at the age of sixteen, it had an exclusively Indian membership. Walking into the little room in Ferguson College, where the society met over tumblers of tea to discuss papers, philosophical and literary, it felt like walking into a meeting of the politburo of the Chinese Communist Party. The average age was rather high.

That first time I attended, some turbaned professor was reading his Ph.D. thesis on an obscure Indo-philosophical academic topic. Most of the other members were asleep. I wouldn't have gone back, except that the lecturer who had introduced me to the society and had adopted me as one of his disciples was to read a paper on linguistic philosophy, in particular the work of an American called Max Black. He insisted that I go, if only to see that the fossils gathered there would never understand mathematical philosophy, his particular thing, or the works of Russell and Whitehead on which he had written his thesis.

He was right. He demonstrated his mathematical contentions on a blackboard and no one in the room least of all myself, understood

a word. Polite questions were put at the end. Did the theory have
applications and so forth. Any of the older members there could
have given my man a run for his money when it came to Aristotle,
Plato or the principles of logic, but semantics, syntactics and the
like were beyond them.

After the meeting my mentor asked me what I thought and, in
the interest of honesty, I told him that I hadn't understood a word
and that his paper hadn't inclined me to correct that ignorance. He
was hurt. We cycled back to the cantonment some miles away in
silence.

A few weeks later he sent word through another of his disciples
that I had better attend the next meeting, if I could force my way in
somehow, because John Wayne was, in a departure from normal
practice, addressing the Poona Philosophical Society.

The news spread through our college like the proverbial prairie
fire of Maoist literature. People who couldn't even spell 'philosophy'
began badgering the likes of us, members of the society, for passes to
the meeting. For a week or so I basked in the glory of membership. I
handed out the passes I had requested from the membership secretary who was himself bemused by the interest shown as he, in perfect ironic reversal, hadn't actually heard of John Wayne.

On the day, the small meeting room had to be exchanged for a
larger lecture hall and the very unlikely audience trooped in. The
turbaned professor brought in Mr Wayne who turned out not to be
the cowboy of the people's dreams, but a Welsh novelist different
and disappointing in every particular even down to the spelling of
his name, which was Wain.

Half the crowd walked out.

Mr Wain spoke interestingly about intellectual assumptions,
East and West, if I remember correctly.

The speech stayed with me and was pleasantly reinforced by the
appearance of a memoir by the same John Wain in a magazine called
Encounter to which our college library subscribed. *Encounter* was
seen by me and by others like me, who were interested in literature

and politics, as a benchmark of interest and intellect at the time. The magazine was edited by Stephen Spender and Melvyn J. Lasky, from London and America, and contained writing from both countries. I first came across Harold Pinter and Angus Wilson in its pages. Mr Wain produced two articles in two successive months about his trip to India.

I remember the articles well. He described Poona University and the college I attended. He was invited to tea at the bungalow of the Principal, Professor P. R. Damle, Professor of Logic, a small man with a fairish sallow skin and a head too long for his short body. Professor Damle always wore a blue suit with sometimes an ill-matched mustard sweater beneath it. He lived with his wife in the little bungalow right in the middle of the campus, a house with a location and size suggestive of a caretaker's cottage.

We pupils never thought that he, his cottage, his logic, his wife or his style of hospitality were worthy of any particular comment. He was a decent man who did a decent job but we had never seen him as the Poona equivalent of Pickwick or Gradgrind. And yet here he was in *Encounter,* written about in truthful and insulting detail. Wain had been to tea with him and found that he could think of nothing but the cockroaches that crawled out to greet him while he was being served tea in a cracked China tea set.

The Welsh writer was overcome by the chagrin and pity of it all. He had read the university's statistics, the number of students, the pass rate, the pressure of a poor population processed through the degree machine by the likes of Damle; he had felt the pulse of intellectual discussion and professorial expertise and he despaired of Poona and all its works.

It was a revelation. He described our college, our town, our Principal. There was nothing in what he said that was unfamiliar to us. What startled us was the presence of these details in *Encounter.* Poona would now be brought to the attention of the audience who normally read Pinter's 'stories'.

The articles made some people furious. Whatever the truth of the matter, however many cockroaches there were in the Damles' bungalow, Mr John Wain should not have written about it. Even the cowboy would have had more respect.

Those articles haven't gone away. The teenage memory remains with me because it was the closest 'literature' came to the familiar and it struck home. In the colonies literature becomes politics, writing takes on the seriousness of a challenge to one's nationality, intelligence, even civilization. It would have been felt in the same way by C.L.R. James's circle of intellectuals who founded *The Beacon.*

The outrage of the Poona philosophers bred a secretive admiration in me for Wain, the ingrate who repaid his invitation to tea with writings in shaming detail. I recognized a kind of truth in what he wrote and the recognition gave me courage. By being unflattering he was making the Indian reader face up to the fact that there were devastating criticisms to be made of how we lived and what we thought. The Wain pieces, the words of a man who was glad to put some distance between his mind and the paucity of our intellectual life, had a suggestion of doom. We were somehow damned.

Later on came *An Area of Darkness* by V. S. Naipaul, a book about his first sojourn in India. Naipaul's observations are summarized in the book's title. It roused its own storm.

Just as C.L.R. explored the books on the shelves of his front room in Tunapuna, I was impelled, on boring mornings in Bombay, on visits to my grandfather's house, to look at the sparse collections of books which he and his brothers had built up. There were two that I was seen thumbing through and both were confiscated. I was forbidden to read them. One was *Mother India,* written by an American called Katherine Mayo. The other, which seemed to be written with the purpose of denigrating Gandhi, was a book called *Judge or Judas* by an English journalist, remembered primarily today for his books on the pleasures of gardens and gardening, called Beverley Nichols.

I was told that Katherine Mayo had been 'sent' by the British to prove to America that Indians were not worthy of self-government, that we were presented in it as a primitive superstitious people who could not be entrusted with administration and the democratic process. The rights that Americans and British enjoyed as politically enfranchized citizens could not be extended to irrational, violent Indians.

Indians had written rejoinders: Lala Lajpat Rai's *Unhappy India,* a nationalist defence and a statement of anti-colonial policy dedicated to the freedom struggle. The other, *Uncle Sham,* was an attack on the United States in the vein of Mayo's attack, full of convictions that had filtered southward from Moscow through Samarkand and the Khyber Pass.

Among the first books to which C.L.R. and his fellow angry young colonials of the early century chose to reply was James Anthony Froude's *The English in the West Indies,* originally published in 1888. Froude, who was a friend of Carlyle and later became Regius Professor of Modern History at Oxford, had travelled briefly in the Caribbean. Based on his short acquaintance, in his book Froude characterized the Negro as an inferior animal in every particular. This attitude, at least among the intellectuals of the Caribbean, was labelled 'Froudacity'.

In his 1969 essay 'On discovering literature in Trinidad: the nineteen thirties'[1] James noted that the ideas of Froude were a kind of corrupt currency. They were still in circulation then, and had never been authoritatively refuted. At the time, however, James and his circle also knew about and acknowledged the work of Jacob Thomas, a nineteenth-century black man who had written a contemporaneous rebuttal of Froude entitled *Froudacity, The West Indian Fable Explained.* This was possibly the first statement with a pan-African consciousness by a West Indian black man and it seems to have caused or contributed to an awakening in James.

Jacob Thomas was a poor schoolteacher who made his way to London in the 1890s with the express purpose of contradicting Froude. He was the first colonial to rebut in detail the view of blacks and colonials perpetrated by visiting writers.

He differentiated between 'intra-African Negroes' and 'extra-Africans', the ten million negroes who lived outside Africa. Thomas's book asked a simple question. Would these negroes outside Africa acquire a distinct consciousness and unite in a 'grand racial combination' or would they fall prey to the corrupting influences of the societies in which they find themselves?

His conviction was that these scattered black people displaced from Africa by slavery would return to it and draw strength and wealth from it, would one day 'conquer'. He initiated the idea of a black diaspora which would one day return to Africa. Marcus Garvey was later to make his own prescription to this black diaspora: 'Get on a boat and go.'

In *Beyond a Boundary* C.L.R. wrote of the effect Thomas had on his own thinking in the twenties: 'It was along these lines that all of us who were black thought. Those who were not black had the same education and were interested in books and music as we were, but they could go elsewhere.'

What James failed to notice or chose to ignore was that part of Jacob Thomas's rebuttal of Froude hinged on his argument that there were black slave owners too, people of colour who owned slaves and small plantations, and that the battle lines were not as clear as Froude made out.

James picked up, rather, Thomas's conviction that the displaced Negroes would one day return to Africa. At this stage, however, he wasn't advocating getting on the boat, except to go to England. James had to journey through the Marxist canon, through the forms of Trotskyism he was to espouse, and through the moral traditions of Western literature, to discover what he felt the association between the diaspora and Africa should be.

Colonial intellectuals, then, had a tradition of sharpening their teeth by sinking them into the hard opinions of imperialists. In this tradition, C.L.R. was an honourable opening batsman. Though the editorial impulse of *Trinidad* and *The Beacon* was literary and cultural, it inevitably turned its attention to politics.

By the time *Trinidad* and *The Beacon* began to spread their influence in the Caribbean, C.L.R. had begun to concern himself with the depiction of society in Trinidad, with the literary perception that would express the life of the island. During this time, while his stories were being published, James conceived the idea of making a living by writing. He gave up his teaching job in 1927 and began to write. While he was working on his first and only novel, *Minty Alley*, he confessed his ambitions to his mother. Discussions ensued, though by this time James had moved out of his parents' house and taken lodgings in Port of Spain, from which vantage point he could survey the foreground of his literary canvas. Was there any money in it, his father asked. Could 'the boy' earn a living through this writing business? He had, of course, read his son's articles in the local papers, but he knew there was not enough money in fiction writing alone to sustain a man and a family in the Caribbean.

His short stories from this time remain as bright examples of the style, purpose and sensibility already developing in James. In October 1927 he had his first literary break with the publication by the British *Saturday Review* of his story 'La Divina Pastora'.

Republished in the *Best Short Stories* of 1928 in England, 'La Divina Pastora' is reminiscent of the style of O. Henry, the American short story writer/convict who unabashedly used coincidence and miracle to make his plots work. It is the story of a young girl on a plantation where beauty withers early under the strain of hard work. In order to secure her lover she sacrifices a gold chain, her only valuable possession, to La Divina Pastora, a Madonna who grants wishes. But the girl's lover is not so much charmed by the magic of the Madonna as made anxious by her unexplained absence from the routines of their courtship. This new, uncomfortable emotion precipitates a decision. The chain reappears on her dresser, miraculously.

About his success with this one story in England, James says: 'If we wanted to write and do something, we had to go abroad. Mendes and I had work published before we left, but that was because distinguished people came to the island, we were introduced to them as "literary persons", and they took our work away and gave it to editors; that's how I was first published.'[2]

No doubt his second published story got into print via the same route. In this story, 'Turner's Prosperity', James tells the story of a clerk who is in constant debt and harassed by his debtors every pay day. Exasperated by the circus outside his business, his employer, a Scotsman, calls the clerk in and asks him to reckon up his debts with a view to helping him out by paying them off. The clerk makes a calculation and in anticipation of this generosity doubles the figure. The Scotsman is appalled and dismisses him on the spot. It is not that the clerk has been caught out in his dishonesty, but that he has miscalculated the tolerances of his employer's generosity. The clerk is dismissed and falls into the abyss.

His third story, 'Triumph', published with 'Turner's Prosperity' in the first issue of *Trinidad*, Christmas 1929, is about the fight for love and survival in the barrack-yard society of Trinidad. Here sex and survival are intertwined. Women hold and lose mercurial men with their wiles, with blackmail, with obeah (sorcery). Mamitz, the voluptuous heroine of the tale, loses her man. She then finds a butcher, a man who can provide. The rivalry for Mamitz's favours breaks into open warfare. Mamitz triumphs in the end when the butcher and his money are won.

James, still in his twenties, was writing with the confidence of form acquired through reading Maupassant and Kipling and with the conviction that the substance and sensibility he was dealing with would be a revelation if not a revolution in English literature. He had few examples to hand of colonials writing about themselves, and fewer examples still of writers inspired by the raw lives of the non-aspiring masses of the empire.

He was not, of course, inventing the wheel. He had before him the short stories of O. Henry who had dealt in some measure with the low life of the American cities. Examples of British writers writing about wretched Victorian Britain abounded and there was, of course, the example of Conrad who stepped outside the geographical boundaries.

James's ambition to be a writer had been growing for some time, and he always spoke of his early writing with some pride. He wrote, for example, for his school magazine, and it gives us an indication of the parochial nature of Trinidad society to learn that these essays became the 'talk of the island'. Perhaps C.L.R. was exaggerating. He may have heard his writing in the school journal discussed by his teachers, his family and a middle class that followed the progress of the promising lads of QRC. Or it may indeed have been the talk of the cricket fields and the market places.

The first of these essays, gleaned not from personal observation but from reports and written in the tone of the humorists of the nineteenth century, was a description of a historic Oxford-Cambridge cricket match. It was a second-hand effort demonstrating the power of parody that a colonial boy could develop rather than any acuteness or freshness of observation.

The second essay was entitled 'Literature as an instrument of reform' and was James's attempt at isolating the social themes of Thackeray and Dickens. The essay was no more than an identification of the cruelty of the school portrayed in *Nicholas Nickelby*, of the state of British jails portrayed in *Little Dorrit* and of the snobbery that characters in *Vanity Fair* manifest. But we can see in this how James's literary mind was developing, and how unsurprising, therefore, it was that, when he turned his pen to fiction, it was the poor who captured his attention.

What created this desire in James to be a writer? Despite the modesty writers affect in public, the ego that makes them want to write has to be consciously fed or stimulated. From where did this urge arise in James? Writing wasn't a substitute for achievement at sport—he was a leading high jumper on the island, captain of the football team and a good cricketer. Neither was he a slouch academically. Although he didn't win the prized scholarship which would have sent him to England and allowed him in due course to return as a colonial administrator, he noted that he did become an intellectual resource for the school. Even as a junior teacher, he was consulted by other teachers and pupils alike on matters of fact, opinion and critical judgement. His theory, which he said was formed early, that one had to know the economic, political and literary phenomena of any time and place to understand its history, put a responsibility upon him.

I am convinced that a certain sort of loneliness nurtured this ambition to write. In all of James's recollections, interviews and writings, there wasn't ever an expression of love for his parents or any hint that real emotion flowed between them and himself. There was certainly respect, sometimes deference and sometimes defiance, but, seemingly, no love. He followed his mother's habit of reading, for example, but never seems to have talked of books with her.

I am also convinced that this isolation of intellectual development is part of growing up in the colonies. There is no surrounding set of values, conversations or inspirations to support ideas. I discovered in conversations with C.L.R., born nearly a half century before me in a distant colony of the same British empire, that we had shared a literary experience. We had both read the whole shelf of Thomas Hardy's novels which we found in a dusty neglected ex-colonial library. We had both discovered an index of dates, and resolved to read the novels in order, from *Desperate Remedies* through *Two on a Tower* to *Jude the Obscure*.

By the time James's first short stories were being published, perhaps, as Mendes says, emboldened by the small income they gave him, James got married.

In 1926 he proposed to a young woman of half-Chinese, half-Creole descent. Juanita was a strikingly attractive girl. James himself curiously wrote in his very rare allusions to her that she was 'the sister of a young woman who was reputedly the most beautiful girl on the island'. Juanita shared James's radical literary and political views such as they were, according to those who remember her; she was shy and spoke very little in public.

The courtship was sudden and short and, even in his immediate circle of literary associates, unexpected. James was in love with the idea of a conquest, rather than with Juanita herself. Perhaps Juanita's sister's reputation as a beauty aroused the acquisitive instinct in James, and not being able to approach the real thing he settled for the more literary sister.

He said in later life that Juanita was a literate and refined person, but he also wrote to the woman who was to be his second wife (Constance Webb) that Juanita was 'a typist by profession'. He leaves it at that, perhaps wanting Constance to understand that she was not really his intellectual equal or companion.

One can only speculate that C.L.R. James was not the kind of character to spare the time to cultivate casual affairs. When he was not playing or watching cricket, he dedicated himself to writing and editing the literary magazines he founded and to the literary meetings and readings that came with the job. If he wanted a relationship or sex, he had to have it within marriage and he had better propose to the girl who seemed to admire him.

John La Rose, Trinidadian publisher and C.L.R.'s friend and junior who emigrated to London in the sixties, recalls that he saw the first Mrs James a few times, years after C.L.R. had left her. La Rose never spoke to her but worked in an office in the building opposite the one in which she worked as a secretary. He describes her as a woman with serene features who wore, on the occasions he saw her, a broad-brimmed Chinese peasant's hat.

Their marriage was, according to James, satisfactory. He says that Juanita satisfied his needs, which were very few. She would cook and keep house, she would act as a hostess to the friends of the literary circle who dropped in. 'There was no snobbery about her', James later said. Towards the end of his life, sitting in his flat in Brixton, he would express some regret that he had not encouraged Juanita to keep pace with his changing life and grow with him.

There seems to have been no deep bond between them. He recalled Juanita saying that the only pleasure he got out of her was when he 'was on top of her'. James had no ambition to raise a family. He wanted to be a writer with all the isolation that the romantic notion of that calling entailed for a young colonial. His marriage was not a miscalculation but seems to have been undertaken without foresight or any care for Juanita's future. His literary ambition at the time was to go to England and redeem in literature the history of his family—a novel he planned—and the story of his island in the form of a call for political and historical justice. Juanita was left behind, at first in imagination and then in fact.

By 1926, the agitation of the unions in Trinidad had carried Cipriani, through the ballot box, into the mayoralty of Port of Spain and then to a seat on the Legislative Council as its first labour representative.

At the time C.L.R. was supplementing his income by giving English lessons as a private tutor. One of his pupils was the Consul General of France, a diplomat closely acquainted with the Governor and a member of the Legislature. The diplomat and James became friends.

Cipriani persisted in his organization of strikes and civil disobedience and his demands for power to be devolved upon the people of the colony. In many ways he had become a nuisance and James was asked by his pupil, the French Consul General, during one of their tutorials, what the population would do if the British Governor of the island arrested Cipriani. Without hesitation James replied that the population would burn the place down. James was sure that the diplomat would report this remark in Government circles and prided himself on the possibility that it had saved Cipriani from arrest.

He may have been right. Certainly, by that time his notoriety seems to have been growing. In 1931, James published an article in *The Beacon* in refutation of an article written by Dr Harland, a professor at the Imperial College of Tropical Agriculture, proving that Negroes were as a race inferior in intelligence to whites: 'I wasn't going to stand for that and in our little local magazine, I tore him apart. I had merely done what seemed to me a routine job, but tinder was around. Students at the Training College spoke to me about the controversy with sparks in their eyes. People stopped me in the streets.'[3]

The article was not merely notorious. It was discussed, said James, in the Trinidad Legislature. His barb had gone to the heart of the system.

Another article, a curious mixture of polemic and fiction, published in *The Beacon* in May 1931, further demonstrates the development of James's political intelligence. 'Revolution' purports to be a report and a conversation between James and a Venezuelan revolutionary exiled in Port of Spain. The Venezuelan revolution against the dictator Juan Vincente Gómez was an uprising of the people with their own generals and troops, with exiled presidents in the story, ships carrying guns, treachery and military encounters within and outside the borders of Venezuela. The short story takes the form of a commentary in a conversational, colloquial, philosophizing style.

The story foreshadows the style, action, concerns and political stance of James's more important work, the history of the slave revolt in Haiti, *The Black Jacobins,* published in Britain in 1938. The form of the story is unusual. James asks leading questions and his 'character' relates the anecdotes, the stories, the history like some Ancient Mariner.

James used the story of Venezuela as a narrative with implicit morals. At one point the narrator talks of the revolutionaries' possible beachhead, an invasionary force:

> There weren't many, no more than a hundred or so, but if they had landed and taken the city and shown they had guns, they would have had a big following at once. All the people would have been with them. All the people are with

us. They are against Gómez. But the Venezuelan is not going to leave his cattle and his wife and children any more until he sees something is really happening. For too many years the revolutionary party in Venezuela has been fooling the people . . .

By using this style of narrative, James was evolving his technique. The common man is the hero. The revolutionary party has let him down. It is not that the people lack 'consciousness' and need it to be raised. They will fight when the possibility of winning materializes.

James humanized his villain. The fact that it was a story forced him to flesh out the characters and their actions. It wasn't cold historical writing, nor was it the great wrestling with abstracts that characterized most left-wing writing in the twenties.

The story was probably drawn from the life and tragi-comic career of Francisco Miranda, the Venezuelan revolutionary adventurer of the early nineteenth century. V. S. Naipaul, probably without any knowledge of James's short story, wrote the history of Miranda himself in *A Way in the World* (Heinemann: 1994).

The final break with Trinidad came about through cricket and James's acquaintance with the cricketer Learie Constantine. Constantine came from a family of cricketers and in 1906 his father had been sent, by the West Indians and by public subscription, to play in England. Constantine, a member of Shannon, the rival team to Maple for whom James decided to play, was selected to play for the West Indian cricket eleven.

Membership of the national side took Learie to Britain and his brilliance on the pitch brought offers to stay there. In 1929 he decided to take up the offer to play for Lancashire in the county championship and remained in Britain thereafter, returning to Trinidad only periodically. On these visits he and James met and discussed cricket and cricketing. Now to their discussions was added 'a new and inexhaustible topic—England and the English people'.

At the end of the 1931 cricket season when Learie Constantine was in Trinidad, according to James 'he exploded'. He said he wanted to write a book, about cricket, about himself and about the British. James agreed to do the writing for him.

Work on the book began immediately. James records that he kept a note pad on his knee to record points from their conversations and he says that he and Constantine were conscious that they: 'were making history. This transcendence of our relations as cricketers was to initiate the West Indian renaissance, not only in cricket, but in politics, in history and in writing.' He need only have added 'and of course in new frontiers of modesty'.

During the course of the meetings James confessed that he intended to go to England and to become a writer. Constantine thought for a moment before saying: 'You come on to England. Don't put it off. Do your writing and if things get too rough I'll see you through.' They agreed to meet the following spring in England.

There was nothing left for C.L.R. in Trinidad. He was tired of the drudgery of his private tutoring and his literary ambitions were bursting the seams of his colonial straitjacket. He had to go to England.

In 1932 it was a bold, indeed wild project, but James's ambition was to be a writer of consequence, a writer like Thackeray, and that was impossible within the confines of Trinidad. Now Learie offered him a ticket to the wider world he must conquer. He was already thirty-two. The offer had not come too early.

3

The Exile Arrives in the Kingdom

The C.L.R. James who left Trinidad in 1932 was an aspiring writer, a player of cricket, a black intellectual heading for the intellectual Mecca of the British colonial—London. He had finished with Trinidad. He had no business there. There was, though, one piece of unfinished business: his wife, Juanita.

When C.L.R. married Juanita, she was not interested in world revolution, but then neither was he. Some years later he wrote to the woman who was to be his second wife about how he had left his first: 'There was some sort of arrangement whereby she was to come to meet me in England, but she saw after a time that I did not really need her and her pride rebelled . . .'[1] He didn't need to finish the sentence. Juanita's pride *had* rebelled. She may have been a comfort in the remote Trinidad days, someone warm to go home to, but she was the wrong woman for a man in search of an international stage. C.L.R. left for England having made 'some sort of arrangement' with his wife. Seven years later she would hear from his American lawyers.

James carried with him from Trinidad the manuscript of a novel and the manuscript of *The Life of Captain Cipriani: The Case For West Indian Self-Government*.

Though he was on his way to a precarious existence by dint of writing, the journey held no dread. In his heart he was convinced that England would not only open the door on his career as a novelist but would give him the opportunity to pursue the political agenda of anti-colonialism. There was the example of Gandhi and the Indian National Movement and his own experience of Cipriani's anti-colonial fight. By his own admission he hadn't the vaguest idea of what form this anti-colonial pursuit would take, or what organizational vehicle it would use. He was only convinced, through his reading of the political journals of the time, that he would find like-minded people.

At the time it struck no one as paradoxical, least of all James himself, that Britain extended a welcome to those of its subjects who expressed virulent hostility to its continued rule of their colonies. Britain had traditionally been a haven for all sorts of dissidence, including that against itself. It was the land that offered those who opposed it the opportunity to agitate, to write and to become famous through that agitation.

British dissidence had created and ensured this enigmatic freedom. Imagine the modern Government of Iran welcoming with open arms and literary prizes apostate authors who had written critically about Islam or the Prophet. Or imagine the regime in China welcoming anti-communists.

Colonial dissidents at the time either came to Britain or went to jail in their own countries. Nehru and Gandhi went to jail. Krishna Menon, the Indian communist who later became India's Defence Minister and Nehru's personal Rasputin, came to Britain and began his agitations in British politics. He joined the Labour Party and stood as a London councillor from St Pancras. It was accepted that the subjects of the British empire could be elected to the British parliament from a British constituency and then use the platform to further political causes much wider than the welfare of their constituents.

Rajni Palme-Dutt and Shapur Saklatwalla, for example, Indian communists and dissenters, enemies of the King Emperor, came to Britain in the first decades of the twentieth century as anti-colonial agitators. Palme-Dutt became a leader of the British Communist Party and Saklatwalla was elected, from the constituency of North Battersea, the first communist MP to Westminster.

James's first forays into London were by no means dissenting. He landed in Plymouth and took the train to London where, through Learie Constantine's friends, he found temporary lodgings in the university area of Bloomsbury. He spent seven weeks in London. Learie was living in the north of England, in Nelson, Lancashire, and James was to go there, but he wanted to stay in London as long as he could afford to.

He began calling on the editors of magazines which had published his short stories while he was in Trinidad and through them acquired a ticket to the British Museum library and an introduction to the literary folk on the fringes of the still influential Bloomsbury circle.

James immediately got to work. He put down his impressions of London in six articles in as many weeks and sent them off for publication in the *Port of Spain Gazette* in Trinidad. These articles about the homecoming of an 'English intellectual' as he described himself, demonstrate more than anything that James was not interested in the architecture of Bloomsbury, nor in the fauna and the flora of Britain. In them he was weighing himself against the authentic avoirdupois of London intellectual life. Their purpose was to measure the authenticity and depth of the culture and education he felt he had painstakingly acquired. He triumphed in the tests. He found himself lacking in no particular and more advanced in most than the people he encountered.

The first essay described his experience of attending a lecture by Edith Sitwell, a lively account of the appearance and conceits of the colourful poet. In the course of her talk she denounced the work of D. H. Lawrence and lavished praise on a 'young American novelist'. James was at pains to tell the readers back home that he alone in the audience guessed the identity of this novelist. When in the later interactive session he put the name Faulkner to Edith Sitwell, he told his readers she was amazed at his perspicacity. Not once but twice during the same lecture he amazed her. When Sitwell dropped a reference to a musician she disdained to name, once again, according to his article, C.L.R. James was the only member of the audience who could put a name to the subject of the anecdote.

The young intellectual was anxious to arrive, anxious to prove to himself and his Trinidadian readers that he was equal to any challenge that the cultural sophistication of London could set him. It was in these essays that his combative spirit emerged and became evident. James seems almost amazed that his small conquest of literary London has been so easy.

He was living on the little money he had brought with him from Trinidad. When that ran out, he would either have to earn some money by writing or take up Learie Constantine's invitation and live with him in Nelson.

After seven weeks, it was lack of money more than anything that made James decide to leave London and make his way to the north of England and the Constantines: Learie, his wife Norma and their young daughter, Gloria.

The Constantines' house in Nelson was small and, years later, James reflected that he might have been a nuisance to the family, a thought that didn't occur to him at the time. Learie Constantine was the most famous black man in Lancashire and very well known throughout the country's cricketing fraternity. 'He was on lunching if not dining terms' with the best of them, is how James put it years later. He knew mill owners, professional men and working men, and was frequently invited to church meetings, to lunching societies and clubs to speak either about cricket or about the West Indies.

To these meetings he now invited James. It was C.L.R.'s opportunity to observe a very different England from literary London and to find a voice in which to speak to it, because soon Learie handed over to James the task of entertaining and instructing these audiences. He would say a few words of introduction and then James would deliver the talk. Learie, James said, would 'sit on the platform listening to what he already knew or had heard many times before with the attention of a man hearing it for the first time.'[2]

As very few people knew anything about the West Indies, inevitably associating the name with India, no doubt James and Constantine spent some time and patience explaining the historic mistake that Columbus had made, and explaining how the descendants of Africans were now known as West Indians. Being Trinidadians, they were also conscious of the confusing fact that a very large proportion of the population of their island was descended from labourers from India itself, distinguished from those of African descent by being called East Indians, but unrelated to the East Indies which were the islands of Java and Sumatra between Asia and Australia.

Definitions done, James would speak to his audience about West Indian society, its sophistication and its political restlessness. He spoke of the anti-colonial ferment in the West Indies, of Cipriani's movement and of the rights and fitness of the people of Africa and the Caribbean to govern themselves. The Labour Party and the Independent Labour Party, separate but related organizations, were active throughout Lancashire and their networks spread the word about this charismatic black speaker. James was invited to Labour Party meetings, clubs and to working men's societies.

In Lancashire, the love of cricket spread across class boundaries and James found himself addressing some political audiences who were well informed about issues of colonialism in the larger colonies. Although the West Indies and Trinidad were not high on their political agenda, they knew about India and had heard of Gandhi and the fight for independence in India. Gandhi had visited the towns of Lancashire and had been given the hearty support of the mill workers. James was addressing audiences who were familiar with this and were in tune with the aspirations of the 'toiling masses'.

Learie Constantine was caught in something of a dilemma. He was a working-class hero, being a black cricketer and a leading player for Lancashire. He was also a social acquaintance and friend of mill owners and landed people whom he met through the upper-class networks that were woven around cricket. In the thirties these two classes were bitterly divided and Constantine, as an outsider and a professional sportsman, was challenged to take sides. If he talked of anti-colonialism the discussions and questions would inevitably lead to questions of social justice and the politics of Nelson, the mills, Lancashire, the Government. He felt he couldn't be seen to back one side or the other in the bitter politics of textiles. It was partly to solve this problem that Constantine left the speaking platform to James.

James began to attend meetings of the Labour Party and of the Independent Labour Party, opposing sides within the labour movement. The ILP was, together with the trades unions, the cooperative societies and the Fabian Society, one of the co-founders of the Labour Representation Committee, which became the Labour Party in 1906. The ILP saw itself as a force for socialism within the labour movement and by the thirties its membership had disagreed with the direction of the Labour Party and had been expelled from it. Many of its members, however, belonged to both organizations.

In the thirties the Lancashire mill workers were amongst the most militant in unionized labour. The General Strike of 1926 was still fresh in the memory. It had divided the nation and given the ordinary citizen new terms for old antagonisms. It had polarized the supporters of workers and the apologists of capitalism. Even those who wavered in between the two poles had learned the language with which each abused the other.

After London and its literary circles, after the middle-class cricketing circles around Constantine, the bluff workers and veterans of Independent Labour Party meetings extended to James a different sort of hand of friendship. For the first time in Britain, it didn't smack of tolerance.

These men knew all about exploitation, or thought they did. They knew all about the history of revolt. They saw themselves as part of the movement that had fought and lost the General Strike. There had been bitterness after the defeat and accusations of betrayal. The more serious 'socialists' had retreated with a determination to study, to bide their time and to build the institutions of the

working class. To them, James was a British subject from an obscure colony who was making a case for its independence. They had
a tradition of welcoming strangers and a tradition of being led by
self-taught men, among whom were communists who had studied
the anti-colonial movement in India. They knew about Gandhi and
were informed about the appeal of the more radical Communist
Party of India to the people of the subcontinent and the people of
Britain. Now here was James arguing that revolution would come
from the colonies. They knew that the colonies were oppressed,
yes, but that they were revolutionary? That could be asserted, but
where was the evidence? Had the colonies produced a revolution of
the peasantry or of the workers? It was a question James had to face
up to.

In this circle, antagonism to the prevalent order was the badge of
courage. James read the political manuscript, which saw West Indian self-government as the ultimate aim of a movement such as
Cipriani's, to Constantine, who offered to pay for its publication if
James could find a local publisher.

James was well connected with such a publisher. He contributed
articles at the time to *Controversy* and *The New Leader,* both publications of the Independent Labour Party.

So, in 1932, *The Case for West Indian Self-Government,* incor-
porating the chapters on the life of Captain Cipriani, was published
in Nelson by Cartmel and Co., a local publishing house. Cartmel
was a very small publisher and James and friends undertook the
parcelling and posting of copies of the book themselves. It was par-
celled off to Trinidad and received favourable reviews there. Copies
were also sent, via friends and political acquaintants, to the radical bookshops of London and other cities.

In Nelson, amongst the Labour Party and those who knew James
and Constantine, the book became a talking point. Meanwhile, the
Conservatives amongst their friends held their peace.

The book quotes Lord Olivier (not the actor Laurence Olivier,
but the Governor of Jamaica at the turn of the century and head of
a Commission on West Indian Government in the early thirties)

who had written a report for the British Government on the people of the West Indies: 'In the matter of natural good manners and civil disposition the Black People of Jamaica are very far, and indeed, out of comparison, superior to the members of the corresponding class in England, America or North Germany.'

That was the beginning and almost the end of James's argument at this point: the ability of the blacks and the arrogance and mendacity of those who ruled over them. Lord Olivier chose the people of 'North Germany' for unfavourable comparison with the blacks of Jamaica, perhaps because in the thirties, when the Nazis were gaining an increasing amount of support in south Germany, this was evidence of north German gentility.

C.L.R.'s friends in the Independent Labour Party of Nelson were more sceptical than the Trinidadian papers in their reception of the book. But James took their scepticism with good humour. In later years he was to say that their grudging reactions to what they saw as a bourgeois theory of politics underpinning the argument of the book began a train of thought in his own mind. These trades unionists and battle-hardened shop floor politicians saw the progress of history in terms of class and the struggle between the classes. They said they found James's emphasis on the 'civilization' of the Negroes patronizing and embarrassing.

Letters and reviews from the West Indies were enthusiastic and kept coming. Constantine's ambition, which was in large measure to use his skills and fame to bring the West Indies to world attention, had advanced by a small step. The London papers didn't pay much attention to what was basically a polemical pamphlet but it was picked up by Leonard Woolf who asked James to re-edit the book and separate the biography of Cipriani from the polemic making a case for West Indian self-government. Woolf published this truncated version as *The Case For West-Indian Self-Government* in his pamphlet series in 1933.

It was, of course, to collaborate on another book that James had been sponsored by Constantine to come to England, and Constantine's *Cricket and I* was published in 1933. The subtext of this autobiography was the West Indian project, which was to publicize the abilities and culture of West Indians, towards the political end of being deemed worthy of self-government. It was a true collaboration and C.L.R. said later that even when it was published he couldn't tell which were his words and which Learie Constantine's. James would listen to Constantine's recollections, ask the relevant questions and then structure the narrative of the chapters. The book had a limited success and was reviewed in the cricket magazines. But by the time it appeared, James's own preoccupations had moved on.

James gave the joint project a boost when he was invited by the BBC to join a panel of speakers on a radio programme which celebrated the centenary of the abolition of slavery. He accepted the invitation and later proudly recalled his first British radio appearance, in which his aim was to make people understand that the West Indians were westernized people. He said that he made his point well, too well, in fact: 'Colonial officials in England, and others, began their protests to the BBC almost before I had finished speaking.'[3]

The broadcast went against the grain. James's views were startling, radical, but why should his assertion that West Indians were civilized have disturbed the Colonial Office? Perhaps because the British public, unfamiliar with the West Indies, had not been exposed to the idea that these colonial societies were westernized, anglicized and deserved to be granted their independence.

James noted with the same innocent pride with which he boasted about the protests that Constantine, his West Indian wife Norma and many friends in the North were listening to the broadcast and 'were very, very pleased'.

While he was assisting Constantine, James was reading voraciously. It was a second period of literary discovery and the first time that James had ventured into political theory in a major way. He was guided by the new friends he had made in the Labour Party and in the Independent Labour Party and by the urge to be armed in his discussions and arguments with them.

In an interview in 1981, James claimed to have been reading at that time Leon Trotsky's *History of the Russian Revolution* as well as the works of Lenin and Stalin. He read *The Eighteenth Brumaire* of Karl Marx and then moved on to Marx's *Das Kapital*.

Curiously enough, however, in a letter to Constance Webb, written after he had gone to live in America in 1938, he proposed that they should read Marx's volumes of *Das Kapital* together and compare notes. He offered to coach her through correspondence as they went along. The discovery that there was not one volume of *Das Kapital* but three animated him. He was sure that very few people who called themselves Marxists knew this, and he resolved to master all three volumes. In effect he confessed here, writing on 24 April 1939, to reading Marx for the first time.

In the years between leaving Nelson and the letter to Constance Webb he had built a reputation as a Trotskyist and a Marxist, had written a distinctive volume on the Russian Revolution, and had lectured in the USA; and yet he admitted that he had just bought his first copy of *Das Kapital* and intended to read it:

> And now for *Das Kapital*. My dear young woman I have some news for you. One C.L.R. James, reputed Marxist, having thought over his past life, and future prospects, decided that what he needed was a severe and laborious study of—guess! The Bible? Wrong. Ferdinand the Bull? Wrong again. Not *Das Kapital?* Right. (Loud and prolonged cheering, all rise and sing the 'Internationale'.) I bought the book a few days ago in pesos and have got down to it. (This is only one volume by the way. There are two more. You made a mistake when you thought you had read them all.) I shall read those three volumes and nothing will stop me but a revolution.[4]

While still in Nelson, James was winging it with the Marxist theory. He didn't grapple with, understand, interpret or indeed contribute to it till years later. The essays and notes he wrote, however, in the 1940s attest to a thorough reading. The serious study had finally begun. His readings in Nelson into the work of Trotsky, Lenin and Stalin acquainted him with the practice, the technology of revolution as it unfolded in the Soviet territories. But as the later confession proves, his reputation as a 'Marxist' speaker and thinker, acquired in Nelson and later in London, was based on intelligent bluff.

James now needed to earn some money, because he knew he could not remain dependent on Constantine much longer.

The opportunity to become self-sufficient came through cricket. He attended a cricket match between Rawtenstall and Nelson, both Lancashire towns, and noted particularly the bowling of one Sydney Barnes. This S. F. Barnes was fifty-nine, a tall man who bowled with a ramrod arm, swerving with power to land the ball with the precision for which James called him the greatest bowler in the world.

James was so taken by the appearance of Barnes and his taking of seven wickets on the day that he saw him that he wrote an adulatory piece about him and showed it to Constantine. Constantine brought it to the attention of Neville Cardus, the cricket correspondent of the Manchester *Guardian*. Cardus liked it and published it and offered James a job covering league matches for the paper in the north of England.

James took on the job with enthusiasm. For the next three cricket seasons of 1933, 1934 and 1935, he wrote reports of the county championship matches for the Manchester *Guardian,* following Cardus's style as a raconteur and critic of the game. James quickly built himself a reputation as a commentator with an unusual insight into the game. His writing would address the personality of the player, batsman or bowler and his reports always seemed to be in quest of narrative and drama. In 1936 he left the Manchester *Guardian* and reported the season for the *Glasgow Herald.* Cricket gave him a very welcome independent income, and it also gave him the opportunity to travel all over England and Scotland.

It was this independent income that enabled him, soon after he had collaborated on Constantine's autobiography, to move back to London.

In London the early 1930s were a time of intense political activity, a great deal of it centred around the magazines and propaganda pamphlets of small political groups, workers' circles, socialist formations and émigré agitators. The journals were full of advertisements for meetings. One could, on any day of the week, attend ten lectures in which the speaker would try to draw the audience into a debate and into a 'cause', and in most cases into a more particular resolve to contribute money and time.

Through such an advertisement in 1936 James learned that 'the famous George Padmore' would be speaking at a hall in Gray's Inn Road. The speaker was billed as an anti-colonial West Indian and, what's more, a Trinidadian. He would be making, the advertisement explained, an explicit connection between the exploitation of Africa and the colonial status of the West Indies, something James had not done in the as yet unpublished manuscript he was carrying with him: *The Case for West Indian Self-Government.*

To James's utter astonishment, 'the famous George Padmore' who took the platform was none other than his childhood friend, Malcolm Nurse. Nurse had come a long way from Trinidad. He had been to the United States and was a member of the Communist Party and a staunch supporter of the Soviet Union. He had even been to Moscow several times for 'training'.

Here was Nurse, under a pseudonym, in the thick of the struggle that James himself had come to England to join. James was overwhelmed.

In an essay written in 1969, James recalled Alfonso Nurse, Malcolm's father, an intellectual of his own father's generation, who according to James had the largest collection of books that James had seen in the Caribbean. The story that James tells in this essay stands out as the one incident of a directly racial nature that he recalls from his childhood. James's family and the Nurses, parents and children, were friends. Alfonso Nurse and James's father were both teachers and both were distinguished by being a part of the black middle classes as distinct from the white and the Creoles.

The story goes back to 1900, to before his own birth. Alfonso Nurse was assigned the post of a supervisor of students of agriculture under Professor Carmody, a white man. A controversy of a scientific nature arose in the newspapers. Mr Nurse, who had read a lot of science, joined the controversy and signed himself 'James Alfonso Nurse, "Agricultural Inspector" '.

Professor Carmody took offence. Who the hell was Nurse, a mere supervisor of student teachers in his department, to pass scientific opinions? Besides, he had no right to call himself an Agricultural Inspector as he was merely a supervisor of the student teachers. The professor publicly humiliated Mr Nurse because there was some literal but ungenerous truth to his objections. Mr Nurse was so offended that he resigned his supervisor's role in the education department and converted from Christianity to Islam, becoming the only Black Muslim in Trinidad.

From a distance in time Mr Nurse may be judged as something of an eccentric, but the story rings true and speaks of the depth of feeling generated by a petty scientific controversy and the teeniest tug on the inelastic protocols of race. It was a controversy between a white man with petty authority and a black man trying to earn some.

After the Gray's Inn Road meeting, James tells us, he and his childhood friend spent the night getting reacquainted. At the age of ten the young James and the young Nurse used to swim together in the Arima river in Trinidad. In the twenties Malcolm Nurse went to Fisk University, Nashville, and then to Howard University, Washington, D.C. He had become by this time a militant revolutionary and abandoned his studies and joined the American Communist Party as a 'paid functionary'. It was then that he adopted the name George Padmore because in the 1930s it was advisable for an

American Communist to try and keep his real identity from the FBI and from rival factions and comrades alike.

Malcolm, whom James quickly learned to call 'George', had been arrested in Germany and jailed by the Nazis for a short spell.

After that night James didn't see George Padmore for a few months until December 1936. By this time James had a flat in London and was becoming something of a figure in Trotskyist circles.

Padmore appeared at the flat pale and drawn and told James that, after twelve years of risky and devoted service, he had broken with the Communist Party.

It was Padmore who now drew James into the Pan-African movement of which he had become a prominent member, first as a spokesman of the Communist Party and now as an opponent of it. It meant, in the abstract, agitating for African freedom and impressing the population of Britain with the arguments for shedding their colonies. In practical terms it meant attending one meeting after another, and keeping abreast of events in Ethiopia, which the Italians had invaded.

To C.L.R., London was at the heart of things. The political demands of the anti-colonials were covered in the papers and came to the attention of the British public and of the Colonial Office, which wasn't thousands of miles away but round the corner. Sometimes, it was said in those circles, they were not round the corner but in the room itself, as it was assumed that Government 'agents' and spies circulated amongst the radicals and kept files on them. They probably did.

In London, James earned his living through cricket, shared houses and flats with various people, all of them activists in the Trotskyist movement and grew increasingly more absorbed with the ILP.

At the best of times, membership of a political party in Britain has never been a very sharply defined business. One fills in the form, pays the subscription and attends meetings. Very often, candidates who stand for office discover to their embarrassment that their membership of the main organization or its branch has technically lapsed or that they don't meet the qualifications set down in some clause of the constitution. So it was with the ILP in those days.

The dominant thinking within the ILP was organized Leninism as defined by Leon Trotsky, and they used the methods prescribed by Lenin in his 1902 pamphlet, *What Is To Be Done*. The first thing to be done was to build a vanguard of committed revolutionaries who would bring out a newspaper which would then spread the 'line'. The Party would take a 'line' on every large historical event and on every important domestic issue, interpreting both as a struggle between the workers and the bourgeoisie.

Using Lenin's prescriptions or despite them, the Russian Revolution had taken place in 1917 and right through the twentieth century the leftists of the world fought over its directions, its rights and wrongs. As the only communist revolution to date in the 1930s the Russian Revolution was taken as an accepted triumph within the ILP, though the Trotskyist line was dedicated to emphasizing the role of Trotsky as a revolutionary leader with paramount military skills. The Trotskyists were dedicated to demonstrating that Stalin had, through a deceptive and ruthless capture of the party apparatus and through assassinations clandestine and 'legal', taken over the party that ruled the Soviet Union. The ownership of the Kremlin was the ownership of the state.

James greedily absorbed the principles of Leninism and, in reading the history of Stalin in the twenties and thirties, was moved to join the Trotskyist 'line'. The Trotskyist 'worldwide' movement consisted in the main of small groups in Europe which had broken away from the communist parties within their own countries and set themselves up in opposition to the writ of Moscow. The Trotskyites argued with the Stalinists and even amongst themselves about the nature of the Soviet Union and Stalin's Government.

Lenin, the technologist and engineer of Marxist revolution, had formulated the idea that the state is a machine that one class uses to oppress the other. James, though he had been a teacher of history had now, through this reading, found a theory of the oppression he had always known needed to be combated. The Trotskyists were embroiled in intellectual formulations of how to demolish the capitalist's state and replace it with a state which would be the instrument of the workers and would dispossess and oppress the capitalist class and any of its remaining lackeys. In the early twentieth century Trotsky had said that the invention of the machine gun had put paid to the idea of revolutions through popular uprisings of people storming the palaces of government. It had to be a more strategic affair than that.

Lenin called his putative state a 'dictatorship of the proletariat'. His formulation elided over the fact that the vast majority of Russia's population and the population of the satellite countries of the Russian empire, the nations of Uzbekistan, Turkmenistan, Kazakhstan and even the countries closer to Europe such as Azerbaijan and Armenia, were almost uniformly peasant. Within the territory of the Soviets was a population of some millions which was in Marxist terms even more primitive: food-gathering nomads. This dictatorship of the proletariat would have to dictate to this majority and, if it resisted, to wipe it out.

Stalin had chosen the path of collectivizing the agriculture of the Soviet Union and at a stroke converting, by an order of the state, the peasants into agricultural workers with a wage paid by the state. The peasants didn't want to be converted into wage slaves and their resistance meant extermination. The peasantry had to be removed in order to create the agrarian proletariat.

This analysis of Stalinism became the bone of contention within Trotskyist circles. A section of British Trotskyists believed that Stalin's betrayal of the revolution took the shape of 'degeneration'; that the Soviet Union had established a Workers' State as Lenin prescribed, but that Stalin had steered it into bad ways.

The opposing sect believed that what Stalin had actually set up was not a workers' state. It believed that he had created a society in which the state, the machinery of class oppression, had taken over the ownership of all capital and had therefore replaced a whole class of capitalists with one single supreme capitalist, more powerful than a fragmented and mutually competitive class. Planning would get rid of wasteful competition and the energies of the nation could be channelled into what Stalinists called 'efficient practice' and Trotskyists called mass slavery. This latter was the description of the Soviets which James held and refined. Stalinism and state capitalism were the enemy.

The practical test of the chasm between the Marxist ideal and Stalinism, the proof of the pudding of these Trot descriptions, was that the relationship between the workers and the owners of the tools, land and machinery with which they created wealth, had not changed. Moreover, the relationship of powerlessness within the process remained as dismal and, in Marx's terms, as 'alienated', as ever.

In later years James went on to base his differences with Trotsky on this very idea of the 'alienation' of labour from the wealth it produces. In the meantime, if a life can be said to have meantimes, he became a supporter of the Trotskyist opposition to the communists and to Stalin.

At this point James was content to denounce the Stalinist tyranny over workers and to adopt Trotsky as the apostle of this opposition. His ability as a speaker had enabled him to rise rapidly among the ranks of the Trotskyist comrades. He joined the ILP's Finchley branch in north London and began to work the circuit.

At a speaking engagement in Glasgow, he came across James Maxton, a dashing radical figure who fancied himself a Scottish Robespierre and cultivated a shock of long black hair and a charismatic if haranguing speaking style. Maxton and his comrades were still obsessed with the failure of the General Strike of May 1926, which the middle classes had broken when, rallying to the call of the Prime Minister Stanley Baldwin and the Chancellor Winston Churchill, they had driven the buses and trains and kept the cities of Britain supplied with food and essentials. The General Strike, which had lasted nine days, had been called in support of the miners who had been confronted by the mine owners with a wage cut, and, when they opposed it, a lockout. In the annals of the left wing the collapse of the strike was blamed on the 'betrayal' of the trades union leadership who wouldn't call for a battle to enforce the paralysis of services.

Maxton, like many others James met through the ILP, was like a man possessed. From him and the others James picked up the real language of class hatred and class war. And while he talked to them, the idea of a literary, historical project was growing. He had to write his next book.

It was through these comrades that James befriended Fenner Brockway, a British radical who lived to become the grand old man of the Labour left. Brockway was a friend of the publisher Frederic Warburg who had, in the spring of 1936, set up with Martin Secker the publishing firm of Secker and Warburg. Warburg was looking for new fiction and heard through Fenner Brockway of C.L.R. James, the Trinidadian writer.

James knew already through publishing his stories in Britain that publishers were more interested in the poor of Trinidad than in the rich. He also knew that exotica was fashionable and that political opposition rather than conformity was the calling card that was welcome in liberal and radical circles. Secker and Warburg set out to publish just such radical and even politically shocking books.

Fredric Warburg wrote in his autobiography, *An Occupation for Gentlemen,*[5] that he was on the hunt for radical writers, was introduced to James and subsequently published *Minty Alley,* James's only novel, in 1936. It was the second book on Warburg's fiction list and though it didn't make a profit and actually lost the firm a small amount of money, Warburg went on to befriend James and to publish his next two books.

Warburg also wrote in his autobiography that Brockway introduced him to James as part of a deal between them. Warburg needed books and fresh thinking; Brockway had friends with fresh thoughts. Some of them were in the Marxist circle, writers in search of a 'committed' publisher.

In the same deal, Brockway proposed that Warburg take on the work of Jomo Kenyatta, of Jennie Lee, George Padmore and George Orwell, who already had a publisher and was well known.

With Fenner Brockway, C.L.R. James and James Maxton, Orwell shared a deep distrust of Stalin and a hatred of his apologists and toadies in Britain.

Through publishing *Minty Alley,* Warburg got to know James well. He watched the writer of this first West Indian novel to be published in Britain transform himself into a political rhetorician. In *An Occupation for Gentlemen* he wrote:

> Despite the atmosphere of hate and arid dispute in his writings, James himself was one of the most delightful and easy going personalities I have known, colourful in more senses than one. A dark-skinned West Indian Negro from Trinidad, he stood six feet three inches in his socks and was noticeably good-looking. His memory was extraordinary. He could quote not only passages from the Marxist classics but long extracts from Shakespeare, in a soft lilting English which was a delight to hear. Immensely amiable, he loved the fleshpots of capitalism, fine cooking, fine clothes, fine furniture and beautiful women, without a trace of the guilty remorse to be expected from a seasoned warrior of the class war . . . If you told him of some new communist argument, he would listen with a smile of infinite tolerance on his dark face, wag the index finger of his right hand solemnly, and announce in an understanding tone—'we know them, we know them'.[6]

To the end, James retained the mannerism of the wagging finger. I remember walking into the flat where he lived in the eighties. It was his routine to ask what I had been up to and what I was going to be up to. I told him I had been asked to speak at a meeting that evening. And who was running the meeting? A magazine called *Marxism Today.* But that, he remonstrated, is *them!*

I knew whom he meant, but played dumb. It was just a magazine. 'No, no, no,' came the reply, 'it is them!' I told him that the invitation hadn't come from the Communist Party but from a group of literary dissenters. Up went the wagging index finger and his eyelids drooped in a pose of infinite tolerance. 'We know them,' he said 'we know them.'

The book that James presented to Frederic Warburg for publication after his open invitation was *World Revolution, 1917–1936*. The European intellectual from Trinidad wasn't going to be just another Trotskyist; he was going to be the foremost one. He had heard argument and disputation. But nowhere had he seen, apart from Trotsky's own publications, a theoretical work which defined Trotskyism, its origins, its critique of the Soviet Union, what precisely it offered the proletariat of the world, and how it differed in its essence and intentions from the communists, the obstacle on the road to revolution.

James wrote *World Revolution* with amazing speed. It was calculated to project him, in less than three years, from a candidate member of the movement into its leading British, if not international, theoretician. It wasn't written as a simple tribute to Trotsky but began with inspirations from Trotsky's critique of the Soviet Union and its degeneration. As subject, James took the events in the Soviet Union and Europe between 1917 and 1936, the year of writing. He went down to Brighton, hired a room in a boarding house and wrote the book in three months. If he had stayed in London, the hectic political life of meetings and speeches that he was beginning to lead would not have spared him the time to write more than speeches and pamphlets. *World Revolution* was published by Secker and Warburg in 1937, the year after *Minty Alley*.

As he wrote, James realized that what began as an explanation of Trotsky's idea of 'permanent revolution' had to end with this clear indication: that where Trotsky disagreed with Lenin, James was on Lenin's side. Nevertheless, James made no open attack on Trotsky. In the tradition used by Marxist writers since Marx, he suggested extensions to Trotsky's arguments. A secretly doubting Trotskyist, even then.

World Revolution is the story of the rise and corruption of the 'Third International' which, roughly speaking, was the group of communist parties at whose centre was the Leninist Bolshevik Party that seized power in Russia in 1917. The hero of the story is Lenin and the genie he commands is the will of the people. It is only when this will of the people is fully manifested in political decisions that the true mettle of the hero emerges. It leads him to victories. When he blunders and neglects to release the powers of the genie, or keeps it in the bottle, the evil magician Stalin, the villain of the piece, takes the stage and plots the confinement, castration and destruction of the genie.

Stalin's manoeuvres in this regard overflowed the confines of the Soviet Union. James justified his grandiose title by outlining Stalin's subversion of the Chinese and German communist movements.

James was not content to rehearse the arguments that other comrades in the Trotskyist movement made against the ideas and dictatorship of Stalin. He wrote his book to project himself as the most serious thinker on these matters in the world. But he was himself amazed at the speed with which this ambition was realized.

World Revolution was the work of an ardent student turned professor. James brought to his task the flair of his literary prose and the conceit of putting the world to rights. The seeming immodesty of the title was, of course, part of the argument. Chapter by chapter, he implemented the Leninist method of taking an issue, quoting someone's point of view and then demolishing it. The point of view quoted was Stalin's, every time, and James demolished it by reference to the first principles of communism. In one chapter James wrote of China and Chinese history as though he had lived with the subject all his life. In truth, like a swot before an exam, he had read it up in days.

The best C.L.R. could say of Stalin was that he had in 1936 withdrawn through his blunders into a position which served as a defence of the Soviet Union but betrayed the workers and peasants of the rest of the world.

Even as he was writing *World Revolution*, James's attention and ambition shifted. His real calling, he felt, was something else. The

Caribbean was a place of transition, not the seat of monarchs, not a place about which anyone wrote histories. He would change this and write a history of the slave revolt of 1789 in San Domingo, the island that is now Haiti. Wordsworth wrote a sonnet about it. He, James, would write its story.

James's new project was a logical progression of his case for West Indian self-government. He would seek out the largest, most significant, most instructive story of revolt in the West Indies and he would write an ambitious history of slavery around it, up to that high point.

Parallel to the French Revolution and in close contact with it, there had arisen in the French West Indian colony of San Domingo a revolt of slaves under the leadership of Toussaint L'Ouverture. The ferment of the French Revolution had reached France's colonies and the slaves wanted liberty, equality and fraternity for themselves. C.L.R.'s book would be the story of Toussaint, a man of middle age when the revolt began, a man who served in the house rather than cutting cane in the plantation; what the Black Power movement was later to call a 'house-nigger'. C.L.R. would begin with the relationship between the slave colonies and the European countries which owned them and fought over them. But dramatically, it would be the story of Toussaint and of the other general of the revolt, Jean-Jacques Dessalines, the militant, uncompromising counterpart to Toussaint's measured strategic approach.

James had to research the interaction of the black Jacobins with the French Revolution, and their subsequent betrayal by the French Republic in France. The French, whose own revolution against the monarchy and aristocracy had begun with their famous cry, had at first encouraged the slaves' revolt and then sent armies to subdue it. The British saw the opportunity the slave revolt offered to acquire a colony and sent a fleet to annex San Domingo. The army of slaves under Toussaint and his slave generals had to fight off both forces.

James made several trips to Paris in 1937 to visit its libraries and museums. The actual writing was done in a rented house in Normandy with the assistance of a young female French translator.

During one visit in Paris, while researching what was to become *The Black Jacobins,* James met Boris Souvarine. Souvarine had been a member of the Central Committee of the French Communist Party, but had been expelled for displaying Trotskyist tendencies. He himself denied being a Trotskyist, and indeed took issue with many of Trotsky's opinions and political positions. Souvarine had written a 700-page tome entitled *Stalin,* in essence a history of the Bolshevik Revolution and an attack on the communists from a democratic point of view. He maintained that the tendency of the Bolsheviks to run a party with military discipline and loyalty stifled all intellectual progress and naturally opened it to domination by a bureaucracy and by a dictator who couldn't be questioned.

James found Souvarine fascinating and accepted a commission from Frederic Warburg to translate the book into English. At the same time, James was making his way in the Trotskyist organization which would have looked upon his association with Souvarine with deep disfavour as Souvarine had dared publicly to criticize the leader. Even in the thirties, any contact with those of opposing views was regarded with suspicion. Friendship with someone of a parallel but opposing persuasion was anathema to Trotskyists, even though contact and friendship with rich sympathizers were treated as an asset. James therefore kept his acquaintance with Souvarine to himself and, even while he was completing the translation, was elected as one of two British delegates to the international conference of Trotskyist parties in Paris in 1937.

Trotsky himself, in exile from the Soviet Union, living precariously as a guest of the Mexican muralist and painter Diego Rivera, issued a statement hoping that this conference would result in the foundation of a 'Fourth International', a union of Trotskyist parties with a common programme.

James addressed the conference on the need for an anti-colonial bureau to recruit members in the colonies and asked the conference to instruct him, as half the British delegation, to set up officially such a bureau. He wanted official sanction and the shelter of the Trotskyist umbrella, though it hadn't withstood any weather yet.

The ILP had broken up over a dispute between pacifists and interventionists when Italy had threatened Abyssinia with invasion in 1935. James had been actively on the side of intervention, which meant implementing sanctions against Italy and sending arms, and when the ILP had given him no viable platform he formed, with Amy Ashwood Garvey, the International African Friends of Ethiopia. James was its chairman. He was joined by his friend George Padmore, and by others like T. Ras Makonen, a British Guianian whose real name was George Griffith.

The Friends advocated the 'interventionist agenda' which meant sending arms and lending military support to Ethiopia. In 1936, when Haile Selassie and his family fled to exile in Britain after the Italian invasion of Ethiopia, James took on the task of explaining and exposing the nature of the imperialist enterprise.

Throughout this period, from the twenties onwards, Marcus Garvey was publishing *Negro World*. Garvey was a Jamaican who had lived and agitated in the US, been expelled from there and landed up in Trinidad. C.L.R. had interviewed him at the time of the longshoremen's strike in 1919 and found him 'an interesting person' but not someone he felt immediately inclined to follow. James had seen copies of *Negro World* but said that he 'wouldn't die' if he never saw another.

James openly disagreed with Garvey's politics in the Pan-African movement he joined in London. C.L.R. and George Padmore went to Garvey's meetings in London to heckle and to siphon off some of Garvey's support.

James later said that Garvey's 'back to Africa' policy was 'pitiable rubbish', but he acknowledged the awakening of consciousness for which Garvey was partly responsible, even though his methods and organization, the Universal Negro Improvement Association, founded in the USA in 1914, were more fascist than socialist. There was no way that the later C.L.R., the theoretician of black revolt, the Pan-Africanist, the man who challenged Trotsky on his analysis of the Negro character could ignore Garvey. C.L.R. knew that himself. His was a voice that was being heard by American and West Indian blacks. But there was no way he could wholeheartedly embrace him either.

Apart from heckling Garvey's meetings there was serious political work to be done. *The Black Jacobins* was published early in 1938, and the next year C.L.R.'s translation of Souvarine's *Stalin* was published in England, Australia and the USA. Its publication immediately after the Hitler-Stalin pact in August 1939 meant that it sold very many more copies than it would have a month earlier. In his memoirs Frederic Warburg remembered that, ironically, had James delivered the translation when it was due instead of months later, it would have been published prematurely and would not have sold as well.

In the 1980s James spoke about these early years in Britain. There were very few black people in literary or political circles in the thirties and he carried the conviction that, as a Negro of the diaspora, he had a peculiar historical destiny. There was, however, a conflict between the writer of fiction and the political agitator and he attempted to resolve this by writing his next agitational book in a novelistic style. He was not ready to surrender the power of the literary for the persuasion of rhetoric. Even then, caught in the dilemma, he was unambiguous about one thing:

> I didn't learn literature from the mango tree, or bathing on the shore and getting the sun of the colonial countries; I set out to master the literature, philosophy and ideas of Western civilization. That is where I have come from and I would not pretend to be anything else. And I am able to speak of the underdeveloped countries infinitely better than I would otherwise have been able to.

We live in one world, and we have to find out what is taking place in the world. And I, a man of the Caribbean, have found that it is in the study of Western literature, Western philosophy and Western history that I have found out the things I have found out, even about the underdeveloped countries.[7]

It was not the simple acknowledgement of a debt. As any other Western intellectual does, he fashioned his own prism through which the 'canon' is viewed. The distinguishing fact of his intellectual legacy was that it owed nothing to Africa nor to any tradition apart from the one which began with the Greeks.

James's assertion was not simply that he, this singular colonial intellectual, was prepared for a life in this tradition. He believed that the whole Negro nation, African and diasporic, had to find a way to live, to understand, and to create within that Western tradition. Because after slavery, that was what the Negro nation of the West Indies and of America had inherited. The conviction born of his own education and observation was not yet allied to any Marxising theory. Behind this conviction was the implicit idea of a civilization and for James the entire edifice of this idea was European, beginning with the classical cultures of Greece and Rome and ending in the literature, art and science of Europe. The black nation of the diaspora was part of this. It just seemed to be a fact.

4

Call Me Johnson

In 1938, his notoriety as a speaker having gone before him, C.L.R. James received an invitation from James Cannon, the leader of the Socialist Workers Party in America, to attend a conference of Trotskyist parties in the United States. He asked for leave of absence from his newspaper job on the *Glasgow Herald* and obtained this, fully intending to return to it.

His books had been received with respect in Britain but hadn't created the sensation that, C.L.R. confessed, he had expected. He had worked at *The Black Jacobins* in the expectation that it would be acknowledged as adding a fresh dimension to European history. It was undoubtedly received as such, but with little fanfare and few sales.

The disappointment must have contributed to his decision to cross the Atlantic, but there was also another reason. During his six years stay in Britain, James had fallen in love with a woman whom he met at left-wing meetings and social occasions. Though protective of her identity, as befitted his idea of gentlemanly conduct, he would in later years say that, 'once we shook hands we never let go'. He cultivated her acquaintance and asked to see her husband in order to confront him with the fact of their adultery face to face. The husband declined to see him and subsequently his offer of marriage was rejected by the woman. James confessed the affair and briefly analysed it in a letter some years later to Constance Webb.

The love affair lasted no more than a year. In writing about it, even about his prospectively bigamous proposal, he never mentioned Juanita, who was still his wife at the time. It was as though she didn't exist. He had moved on to more sophisticated women, members of the Labour movement, women with ideas who commanded and projected admiration.

Yet another factor contributing to James's willingness to leave London was his confidence that, having written *The Black Jacobins,* which was reviewed favourably in *Time* magazine, he had an exclusively powerful grip on what would become 'the Negro question', the political perspective for the self-emancipation of the black population of America.

Plans were made, therefore, and he told Learie Constantine that he'd be back in a few weeks. Constantine asked him if he had the right clothes, since he would be representing the West Indies in the wider theatre of America. Of course James didn't have the appropriate clothes for this lay-ambassadorial task, so Constantine fitted James out with a suitable wardrobe.

C.L.R. landed in New York in October 1938, was received by the comrades and immediately wafted on to a platform to speak on the 'European situation'. His sweep of historical reference and grasp of the situation astonished his audience. Even the intellectuals present had heard nothing like it, and certainly nothing approaching such oratory from the mouth of a black man.

His speech was sharp, analytical, explanatory, full of wit. If the predominantly Jewish New York audience of comrades had ever heard a black man lecture, it was in the tradition of the southern preacher, so powerfully embodied in later years in the rhetoric of Martin Luther King. This black man, this C.L.R. James, spoke in a different idiom. This fresh and unexpected voice expressed itself in a tradition which was descended from an English literary education and from the nuance and understatement of English debate.

The allure of this particular speaker from Britain couldn't be ignored. James was, without a day's rest, sent off on a tour of the United States, by car and train from town to town, wherever the Trotskyists had a caucus or following. He was billed as speaking on the European question at meetings, publicized in local libraries, in the Party's newspaper and on campuses, through which the Socialist Workers Party attempted to recruit new members. It was a punishing schedule of party gatherings, but C.L.R. made a point also of introducing himself to the editors of the national black publications, among them the *Pittsburgh Courier,* which was, according to him, 'the second most influential black newspaper' in the United States.

It was at a public meeting in Los Angeles that James met Constance Webb, who was there with her husband. James and Constance talked and danced at a social function after the meeting and thus began a correspondence of many years, with a three-year gap between 1940 and 1943. At first the letters were about politics, but after 1942 they concentrated on critical thoughts about plays. Throughout the correspondence, James wooed this woman, even though he met her for only a day or two in Los Angeles. They were not to meet again until after the war, in New York, when Constance agreed to become his wife.

During the tour, James realized that the Trotskyist party had no view of the Negro question at all, apart from a vague and fanciful formulation of a 'black-belt' nation, a collection of states with large black populations forming their own country. It was a primitive and uninformed view, a mechanical and arithmetical one.

James immediately observed that he was one of the very few black men in the Party, and the only one who was trusted to speak on its behalf. He began formulating his own task as carrying the burden of the Negro question. His vision was simple. The blacks of America were more motivated towards revolution than any other section of the population, but they wouldn't join the Trotskyist party in order to ensure its success. If they were to join the Party it would have to be led by them on every question of black democratic rights because the black population he encountered was strong-minded and quite determined to act on its own. The blacks wouldn't come spontaneously to the Party; the mountain would have to go to Mohammed.

Trotsky heard of these speeches and invited C.L.R. James to Coyoacan in Mexico where he was living in exile. In April 1939, James set out to meet him.

Trotsky, the co-founder with Lenin of the Bolshevik Revolution of October 1917, had been hounded out of the Soviet Union by Stalin who had virtually grabbed power. With his two sons and his wife Natalya, Trotsky had fled Russia and sought refuge in Turkey. Stalin issued orders to have him killed. Under the threat of execution and pressured by governments who did not want to earn the displeasure of Stalin, Trotsky moved from country to country and obtained entry to Norway. Here, after a while, he was put under house arrest.

Trotsky couldn't or wouldn't seek the protection of his old enemies, the capitalist countries of the West. Then in 1937 he got an invitation from Diego Rivera to live under his protection in Mexico. Trotsky had little option but to accept the invitation.

When James met him, Trotsky was living in a house owned by Rivera and his wife, the painter Frida Kahlo. Rivera had been for years a member of the Communist Party of Mexico but had quarrelled with them over the nature of the Soviet Union, which he had visited and where he had felt snubbed by Stalin.

Another muralist and comrade in the Mexican Party was David Siqueros who was instrumental in expelling Rivera from the Party and precipitating Rivera's revenge, which took the form of inviting the 'red rag', Trotsky, into the country and into his own home.

Trotsky's stay in the Casa Azul was a peaceful one until he, the middle-aged leader of the alternative world revolution, had an affair with Frida Kahlo. Rivera discovered the affair, threw Trotsky out of his house and withdrew the protection that his (Rivera's) prestige, political acquaintance and power of patronage gave him.

He demanded a divorce from Frida, regardless of the fact that he was himself an unrepentant womanizer who had had an affair in the recent past with Frida's younger sister.

James's visit to Trotsky followed this demand for his expulsion from Rivera's house and, though Trotsky hadn't moved out yet, it was known that he would be taking up residence in another fortified house in Coyoacan. Rivera had threatened Trotsky with exposure of the affair, conducted while Trotsky's wife Natalya and their son were living with him. Rivera didn't carry out his threat, but the scandal reached the newspapers and was the talk of Mexico City.

James alluded to the affair in a letter he wrote at the time to Constance: 'I have not met Diego. There is a split between him and L. T.; L. T. is moving out of his house. There have been letters in the press and a general mess. D. R. has left the IV [the Fourth International, the collection of Trotskyist parties round the world].'[1]

James found Mexico 'fascinating . . . poor and dirty, with some tawdry finery but full of life and colour and vitality'. He complained about stomach trouble and about having lost his green pen. He went to see Diego Rivera's murals in the national palace but not much else in the way of tourism. He was after all on an important mission.

James's meetings with Trotsky were unaffected by the scandal and tension in the Rivera/Trotsky household. He found 'the old man' a 'remarkable personality and a very great orator'. Even in ordinary speech, James recorded, Trotsky was 'the great orator personified'. They began by discussing 'the Negro Question'. They agreed on the proposition that the Negroes of America were the most exploited section of society and that without them there could be no meaningful revolution in America. Taking it for granted that their Party would lead this revolution, they then asked themselves why there weren't any Negroes in their Party in the US.

James outlined a series of steps by which Negro writers would be recruited to write for the Party's papers and publications and would record the acts of dissent and revolt evident amongst the Negro population. He also sought Trotsky's blessing for the setting up of a Negro section in the Socialist Workers Party and won it.

Reading the transcribed dialogue of the meetings, minuted by Trotsky's secretaries, we see James seeking the leverage that Trotsky's endorsements would give him in the Party. Trotsky himself, who had probably never met any Negroes outside the hard covers of history books or of *Uncle Tom's Cabin,* was enthusiastic about trusting Comrade James to set up the black section and nurture it under the guidance of the Party. If the Negroes wanted 'self-determination', said Trotsky, then the Party should consider it. But they shouldn't advocate it as their plan or policy. What shape this self-determination would take, whether all the black people of the USA would move to territories of their own and form an independent belt of black USA, or whether they would do something else, was not discussed.

The factionalism of the Trotskyist movement was evident even in this first and only meeting. From Mexico City on 15 April 1939, James wrote to Constance Webb saying that there were now three positions evident in the Trotskyist movement. There was the one he held. Another was the official line of the Party and Trotsky himself, and the third was held by 'the editors of the New International and the French Quatrienne International'. According to James, Trotsky didn't understand the basis of Trotskyism; James did.

This game of dissent from a fixed position would be played over and over again within the Trotskyist movement across the world; moves on a chess board with the players believing that a 'correct line', a more accurate Marxist interpretation would, in the end, bring the masses to the side of the formulators. The 'line' would bring the people, as pollen brings bees. The people bring power. It is the self-persuasive dream of the ultra-rational democrat.

James returned to New York, by boat to New Orleans, and then via Memphis and Washington. His discussions with Trotsky had supplied him with a role. He was to open up the Socialist Workers Party to the Negro population and make it the political vehicle they had been waiting for. James busied himself making contact with Party cadres sympathetic to his line of approach and, at the Party's convention later that year he was able to put through a resolution which stated that the Negro population was 'by their whole historical past to be, under adequate leadership, the very vanguard of the proletarian revolution'.

To make this resolution a reality, the Party set up its Department of Negro Work. Signing himself J. R. Johnson because of his uncertain immigration status, which gave him no right to work, James began writing a column on the Negro question in the Party's newspaper, *Socialist Appeal*.

In August 1939, the Hitler-Stalin pact, a ten-year non-aggression treaty, was signed by Ribbentrop and Molotov. The communist parties of the world, under instructions from Moscow, welcomed the pact. It was left to the Trotskyists to scream dissent on behalf of the world's workers. The pact was seen as a betrayal, an agreement with the worst dictatorship that capitalist society had thrown up. The Negro question became a secondary issue in the Socialist Workers Party and James was put to work producing a pamphlet and writing articles in opposition to the pact.

It was a difficult task. While the Party did not approve of the Hitler-Stalin pact, it was opposed to the war and publicly campaigned for the United States to stay out of it. Workers of Germany should not fight the workers of the rest of Europe and America but rather should unite to overthrow the bourgeoisie. James put all his skill into arguing this point without the least irony, not looking up for a moment to see whether a procession of pigs was moving up ahead on wings.

On September 1 1939, war broke out in Europe, when the Nazis invaded Poland. The Party, with only about a thousand members in the whole of the United States, was thrown into confusion. The leader of the Party, James Cannon, supported by Trotsky himself, was ranged against a faction of young comrades led by Max Shachtman and Martin Abern in a dispute which was not, as might be expected, about whether to enter the war or not. The dispute seemed to be about how to describe the Soviet Union.

Both factions seemed to think that if they could define the Soviet Union and decide whether it was really a workers' state, then they would know what to do about the war.

Both factions were also against Stalinism and the Russian Government. Trotsky and Cannon took the more generous view that the Soviet Union was a revolutionary country under a corrupt leadership. Trotsky still hoped Stalin and Stalinism would one day be defeated in Russia and that there would be a call for Trotskyists, if not Trotsky himself, to take charge again.

James sided with the Shachtman-Abern opposition which carried the young members of the Party with them and was dubbed the 'children's crusade'. They believed that the Soviet Union was not a socialist state in which the workers had seized power, but it was instead a vast capitalist enterprise run by the state.

Instead of the corporations and international companies that ran Europe and America, Russia had a single 'state capitalist' enterprise with totalitarian control over its workers. The faction argued that within the Soviet Union one could see the strains of capitalist production as anywhere else, except that there they were more severe; the Soviet industrial and agricultural workers refused to produce to targets set by the Government, and the country was subject to shortages of food, famine and to Stalinist terror.

While participating in this factional dispute, James was still waiting for the Negro Bureau of the Party, an anticipated official Party organ and a development on the Department of Negro Work, which Trotsky had agreed to set up, to be funded and established. It was his ambition to run it, shape it and make it his own power base. In none of this, however, was he driven by any ambition for leadership, for if he had wanted to be a leader, the way to the top of the Party was clear. What he wanted was for the Negro Bureau to attract hundreds and perhaps thousands of members, and he grew impatient with the ramshackle nature of the Party's administration.

In his letters he was scathing about the bad timekeeping and the sloppy administration of the 'Bolsheviks'. He wrote to Constance Webb: 'When I am dictator, my dear Connie, 10 o'clock will be the deadline for these dear Bolsheviks. I was trained in the bourgeois world, and the haphazard methods of some of these gentlemen amaze me. That is not the way to run a headquarters . . . an office must be run properly.'[2]

The hope of establishing the Negro Bureau as a paying, employing, publishing office and thinking caucus receded. The party continued in serious conflict. The Cannon-Trotsky majority called their opponents 'irresponsible, jittery and unprincipled, subject to social-patriotic pressure'—an allusion to their anti-Russian-communist stand. The opposition called Cannon and his supporters 'Stalinist, bureaucratic and unable to lead the Party'.

From these positions there could be no retreat.

Nevertheless, on 22 October 1939, the Party entertained the 100 or so members at a gathering of the branch, and they netted $25.00.

At the time, James was living in Upper Manhattan in a cold-water tenement room. According to Stanley Weir, then a sailor and a regular visitor to the flat, later a publisher, it was full of newspapers from all over the world. James would read them and mark sections and annotate the articles he was writing. Grace Lee, a member of the Party who subsequently became James's great friend and collaborator, would type the articles sitting at a desk yards away.

It was at this time, while he was writing the pamphlets, that there was a visit to the New York offices of the Party by the US immigration department. Immigration officials were looking for James. He hadn't bothered to regularize his stay in the States and his six-month visa had long expired.

In early December he wrote to Constance who was still in LA:

> Quite a crisis, not political but personal. I have had to leave the office and go into 'retirement'. But I shall carry on from there, and hope for the best. Write to me, will you? Write to Bill Peterson. 116. Enclose the letter in an envelope marked

Goldberg. It will come to me. Write to me as Bill . . . Meanwhile, just say nothing to anybody . . .

He expected Constance to read between the lines. C.L.R. wasn't
going anywhere. He was just beginning his adventure with the
United States and he was going to stay, even if it involved dodging
immigration department officials and going underground.

The cloak and dagger stuff was necessary, even if only because
some lazy bureaucrat had been put in charge of tracking down this
antiwar speaker. He always had the option to return to England or
even to go back to Trinidad, but James had decided that his work
was in the USA. He had become the man who seeks the bleakest
challenge—a West Indian black man opposed to a war; the spokesman of a tiny party that was fatally split on definitions, and a man
with no fixed income, relying on the Party for sporadic payments
and on 'friends' and comrades for subscriptions to his work.

He never seemed to have money, and while complaining about
this state of affairs in his letters, he didn't make heavy weather of
it. James had no grain of self-pity. He handled poverty, when it
overtook him, as it did several times, with a shrug, with humour
and determination. The next post would have a money order from
London. James had become a political Micawber.

The split in the Party continued to widen and by early 1940 the
'children's crusade' had broken loose of the Socialist Workers Party
and formed its own organization called the 'Workers Party'. The
reasoning behind the new name was that 'socialism' as a concept
was unappealing to the American worker, tainted with the rhetoric
and lies of the Communist Party. Nevertheless the American working class was more aware than any other that the capitalist sold the
fruits of their labour for a profit. They would have no problem
identifying themselves as 'workers'.

That was the theory. The truth, of course, was that the workers
of America didn't give a damn what the Party called itself. They
wouldn't come to it.

Even though at the time James didn't quite formulate, or even admit to himself, this futility, his adherence to the rebel tendency, the one which disowned the label of 'socialist worker', was a step towards the realization that the worker of the world was not motivated by reading Lenin but by the injustice of his or her own condition. But James was still with a party or group which felt that the 'worker' would need the guidance of those who had read Lenin— himself and his friends—to drive the revolution forward.

Just before the Party split, James wrote a seventeen-page essay called 'Origins of the crisis' to be circulated amongst the membership. In this he criticized the Party for its futile mimicry of Bolshevism and its search for the 'correct' line rather than trying to expand the membership and gain political influence in the real world. This essay, though it was never intended as more than a corrective, projected James into the leadership of the rebels and when the split came he was seen as one of the guiding intellectuals of the new, breakaway formation.

James began to work for the new dissident Party in earnest. He travelled to Chicago, San Francisco, Washington, wherever the Workers Party had a group. They started a paper called *Labour Action* and James wrote articles countering the lobby that was in favour of entering the war, the Republican and the Democratic press.

He wrote his last columns for the *Socialist Appeal* in February and March 1940. One of these, on the Ku Klux Klan, celebrated the fact that Miami Negroes took up guns to combat intimidation by the Klan who were attempting to prevent them from going to the local polls. 'The Negroes sat in their houses waiting for the Klan with loaded Winchesters across their laps. Backed by this not-to-be despised argument, American "democracy" won a small victory.' Did this advocacy foreshadow the stance of the Black Panthers twenty-five years later?

On 21 August 1940 news came through that Trotsky had been murdered in Mexico by Ramón Mercader, a Spanish adventurer who had inveigled himself into the old man's presence on the pretence of asking his opinion on a piece he had written, ostensibly for the Trotskyist movement. Mercader stabbed Trotsky several times with an ice pick in the back of the head. Trotsky was taken, unconscious, but near death, to hospital.

James wrote to Constance that very day:

> I came here [to Washington] on business and after a meeting last night, and a long talk with the friends, went to bed happy. Now this morning this awful news. It is the greatest blow we have ever received. One by one they have struck down all our best people and now the old man himself. The news is bad, but if he regains consciousness at all and can fight, he will fight for his life. He has always fought for what he thought worth fighting for.[3]

Soon after, Trotsky succumbed to his wounds.

At the time James was himself suffering from an ulcer. 'I must get rid of my ulcer,' he wrote to Constance, 'or it will get rid of me.' He went into hospital in October and, after two months of treatment, emerged, having decided, with the support of a second medical opinion, against an operation.

He threw himself back into relentless political work. With Raya Dunayevskaya, a Russian émigré who had briefly been Trotsky's secretary in Mexico and had been active in socialist politics since the 1920s, James formed a study and discussion group.

This new partnership of Dunayevskaya and James becomes known as the Johnson-Forest Tendency, 'Freddie Forest' being Dunayevskaya's pen name. The partnership was soon joined by Grace Lee, the young Chinese-American philosophy graduate of Bryn Mawr, daughter of a rich hotelier and restaurant owner, who had originally helped James in Manhattan in 1939 and who would remain in active collaboration with James until 1965.

After coming out of hospital, and exhausted by travelling, speaking and writing for the Workers Party, James went for a few weeks for rest and recuperation to his ex-pupil and friend Eric Williams, by then a lecturer at Howard University in Washington, D. C. He felt like a frontline soldier on furlough. He had been working hard and he was beginning to feel the strain.

On the way to the formation of the new Party, James lost a comrade, one James Burnham, a teacher of philosophy at New York University and one of the intellectuals who had engineered the Party split. Burnham was a close collaborator of Shachtman and with him had written a book about the dereliction to the right of the able intellectuals of America entitled *The Managerial Revolution.* With Shachtman he provided the intellectual fuel for the split but, just after it was declared, Burnham went into hiding. He didn't telephone the new Workers Party and he didn't show up at meetings. James's version of events, in his letter to Constance Webb, written, incidentally, on his 39th birthday, casts light on his own view of the passions and needs of a left-wing intellectual:

> Nothing became him less than the manner of his going. He stayed away for weeks immediately after the split—just didn't even come around or phone. Then he turned up with the most godawful document you ever saw. He didn't believe in marxian economics, he didn't believe in the Marxist theory of history, he didn't believe in the party, he didn't believe in Socialism, he disavowed everything he had preached for five years. Reasons? None. None at all. Theories he had taught for five years he dismissed in three lines. Now, my precious, I know Mr James B very well. He is an intellectual of intellectuals . . . A man of remarkable intellect and great strength of character . . . One thing could have saved him. If he had fallen head over heels in love with a woman in the movement, whom he would have followed around, who would have made him enter into the spirit of party life, who would have given him some emotional personal interest in the movement, apart from his intellectual convictions. But

poor man, he loved his wife, I think, and therefore always
remained a stranger to the party . . .[4]

There are two stories here, that of Burnham who wouldn't take
the time to compose a proper rationale for abandoning his friends
and beliefs, and that of James who was trying to convince Constance of the romantic needs of the left-wing intellectual.

The 'crisis' in the Party and the defection of Burnham and others
threatened the organization to the point of disintegration. James
was called back from his 'holiday' with Williams to active duty
with the new Party. Now for all official purposes, he changed his
name to J. R. Johnson.

On 22 June 1941, when Hitler invaded Russia, the Communist
Party in America switched sides. Having previously campaigned for
the US to stay out of the war, their small industrial base was now
put on alert to avoid strikes and contribute to the war effort in line
with the industrial policies and propaganda of the Roosevelt Presidency. The Trotskyists and James remained opposed to the war and
denounced the communists for their volte face.

The liberal pacifists and intellectuals who still professed themselves against the war and argued to keep the United States out of it
were attacked by the 'loyal' press and politicians as Nazi sympathizers. Their position became increasingly untenable. The anti-war
voices faded away, leaving very little organized opposition to the
war. The Trotskyists in theory took up the challenge.

There were too few of them to make much of a difference. The
country was being spurred on to greater and faster production to
serve the war effort. The country was being prepared psychologi-
cally and industrially for entry into the war, but the spurt in industrial production and in the growth of the arms sector meant that
blacks and women, hitherto locked out of waged employment,
were given access to it. There was a significant migration of black

workers from the South to the northern industrial towns and into the factories before December 1941, when, after the Japanese attack on American warships in Pearl Harbor, Hawaii, America entered the war.

This wartime migration contributed to a more volatile labour force prone to unofficial lightning strikes and shop-floor protests against differential pay and treatment. The issues were clear. The war gave employers the excuse to impose a wage freeze and the shortages, natural or artificially caused by hoarders and black marketeers, had forced prices to rise. The entry of blacks and women into industries that had previously kept them out gave rise to friction between blacks and whites and became the natural theatre for equal-pay demands for women. Conditions were ripe for James and his comrades to exploit, but they didn't have the forces to do very much. The ranks of the Trotskyist movement consisted largely of ageing Eastern European immigrants and dissenting young urban intellectuals.

As J. R. Johnson, James had a paradoxical position to advocate. On the one hand, the Party hated Hitler and Stalin, and, on the other, it urged the workers to stay out of the war and hamper the Government's declared determination to defeat Hitler and keep Stalin in check. They advocated the overthrow of their own government, which in wartime was treason.

J. R. Johnson's essays of the time were directed towards the Negro population and in particular he opposed the black nationalist contentions of the ever-influential *Pittsburgh Courier*. The *Courier* contended that black people all over the world ought to wait for the war between the white imperialists to be fought and then pick up the spoils. But, as Johnson pointed out, the Negroes of America would not be allowed to stand aside. They would bear the brunt of the war, laying down their lives for a country which didn't allow them the simplest democratic rights.

When Russia had invaded Finland early in the war, the *Pittsburgh Courier*'s columnist, P. L. Prattis, had pointed out the hypocrisy of the West, which shed crocodile tears for Finland, having stood by when Ethiopia had been invaded by Italy three years earlier. In the *Socialist Appeal,* Johnson had replied with a rather more subtle sermon. The workers of Europe had been ready to defend Ethiopia, Johnson claimed; it was only the governments of Britain, France, Spain and Belgium who wanted to share the spoils with Italy and the communist leadership of the trades unions and workers' organizations which prevented them.

James and his comrades had the difficult task of persuading the American citizen that Stalin's Russia was not really 'communist', that it was in all but name a totalitarian capitalist state. At the same time they had to convince the same citizen that 'socialism' was a good thing and that America really needed it.

James's contribution to this effort was directed towards the negroes. In a pamphlet entitled *My Friends, A Fireside Chat On The War,* published by the Workers Party (June 1940), he argued that the Negro had been denied democracy in the US by the very men, President Roosevelt included, who now wanted to send him to fight. The pamphlet assumed the voice of an old Negro: 'I went to the last war. I was treated like a dog before I went. I was treated like a dog while I was there. I was treated like a dog when I returned. I have been played for a sucker before, and I am not going to be played again . . .'[5]

The writer, of course, hadn't been to the war or been 'treated like a dog'.

In early 1941 James was still suffering from his dormant ulcer. He also suffered from a nervous disorder which made his fingers shake and made writing difficult, something he deeply resented. Despite this, at the end of 1941 he undertook a tour of the South for the Party and in early 1942, together with other members in the South, threw himself into a sharecroppers' strike in Missouri.

The black sharecroppers, who were paid a dollar a day to harvest the cotton they grew on behalf of landlords, were demanding a living wage. They wanted 30 cents an hour—not an extravagant demand, considering how substantial the profits were. The landlords offered them a dollar a day and raised it to a maximum of $1.75 in regions where the workers were more united. James called the black sharecroppers together and in classic agitational style wrote for them a pamphlet spelling out their demands to circulate to a wider audience.

It was good pamphleteering, calling on the white sharecroppers to join the blacks and on the churches to support the strike in language that resonated with the cadences of the evangelical South: 'If a preacher is not with us he is against us. That is the voice of Scripture. Also the Laborer is worthy of his hire. That is Scripture also. We are worthy of 30¢ an hour. God helps those who help themselves.'

According to Paul Buhle, James spent most of his time in St Louis and only occasionally made forays into the countryside to gather material for his pamphlets. He did very little agitation and certainly wasn't inclined to share in the marching and picketing.

At the end of the strike, which the sharecroppers won, James returned to New York. At the end of the year he collapsed in the street. His ulcer was perforated and he had to undergo an emergency operation, for which his friends and patrons, Fredy Drake Paine and her husband Lyman Paine, paid for. They had paid for his earlier hospitalization and they now invited him to recuperate in their house 'on the water' in Long Island.

Apart from being a prominent and gifted architect, Lyman was a political enthusiast. The Paines not only invited C.L.R. to live in their house but encouraged him also to run a salon which integrated their political preoccupations with literary pursuits. Around their house in Long Island and James, grew a circle of intellectuals, mostly women, including Dunayevskaya and Grace Lee. Throughout his stay in America and for years after, the Paines provided him with money, and in the American years a base from which to operate.

It was now, during his recuperation period that C.L.R. became a movie addict. He began with a contempt for the populist form but was soon drawn by the popular mythologies that cinema created to captivate the emotional impulses of the people. He saw the same films three and six times. He admired musical comedies and made little distinction between the good and the trashy.

His theory of film, formulated at the time for Constance Webb, was simple: Hollywood gives the workers the adventure, freedom, emotional extravagance and the drama they lack in their productive lives. The films were myth but possible myth, extensions of reality. 'That is the complete secret of the Hegelian dialectic,' said James, not entirely frivolously. 'The two, the actual and the potential, are always inseparably linked; one is always giving way to the other. At a certain stage a crisis takes place and a complete change is the result.'

In the content of Hollywood films James had discovered the yearnings of the American people. The films were successful because they encapsulated the drama of everyday life and made it into myth. James saw in Humphrey Bogart and Charles Laughton, in Greta Garbo and Clark Gable, the studies of American personality that were completely lacking in the 'political' discourse of the comrades. Of course these films were not intellectually respectable at the time, but James's instinct was in their favour. The films were teaching him about the need for escapism. His training had taught him that Eisenstein, Chaplin, the classics of cinema, could be venerated and he wrote about these as the new art forms of the century. But in his heart he wasn't for Eisenstein at all. He was for Clark Gable. He fell for the drama of *Gone with the Wind*. He loved it.

In one of his last letters to Constance he wrote of a soap opera on television whose name he neglects to mention, which depicted a family during the Second World War. The plot had bathos, the genre was openly commercial, but James could see the mass appeal in the simple sufferings, longings and temptations of the women left behind while their men marched off to war. The ideology of his anti-war stance, formulated at such great length in his essays, was put aside or ignored. The populist in James applied what he knew to these simplicities. The Shakespearean critic, the reader of

Melville and Thackeray, began to see Aeschylian characteristics in the Hollywood movie and the trashy TV drama.

A few years later, between 1949 and 1950, when James's income had dried up and he had Constance and the child to support, he planned and began writing a book on American civilization. It was the sum of his critical appreciation of American popular culture. The manuscript, comprising eight lengthy essays, was not published in his lifetime but posthumously in 1993 by Blackwell in the USA and England. It was called, simply, *American Civilization*.[6]

In the book James explains his intellectual transition from the politics of small groups to his conviction that, through its addiction to popular culture, the mass of people in America were implicitly indicating the aim and direction they wanted from politics.

After years of waiting in vain for the masses to join the Marxist parties and factions to which he belonged, James set out to discover the reason for their tardiness. He started with a fundamental question. If the people don't want the prescriptions of the Trotskyist groupings, then what is it they want?

'Without the answer to this,' he wrote, 'most of the analysis of politics in the United States is not worth the paper it is written on.'

> That 'full employment', 'better working conditions', 'more leisure', 'security' is what the people want—this is a doctrine that reduces mankind to the level of horses and cows with an instinct for exercise. It would astonish the proponents of these doctrines if they really were able to give everyone 'full employment', 'security', etc. It is then that social crisis in the United States would assume the outline and proportions of a gigantic nightmare.[7]

Popular culture became for James the key to a new politics. If one understands why the population worship Bogart and Garbo and in their millions read the novels of Frank Yerby and manifest an addiction night after night to detective plays on the radio, then one can answer the question 'what do the people want?'. Without the answer there can be no political formulation.

James read the novels of Frank Yerby and found them very badly written. He listened to detective plays on the radio and he produced an analysis of Dashiell Hammett's *The Maltese Falcon,* setting out to explain why a cynical detective had captured the imagination of the American people.

It was in the 1940s, while James was writing for the Workers' Party publication, *The New International,* that he began what he considered his most important theoretical work.

The Johnson-Forest Tendency—James, Dunayevskaya and Lee—began, as the war ended, to grow more and more critical of the direction which the Workers Party was taking. The end of the war, the treaties of Yalta and Potsdam, initiated the beginning of the Cold War. The Jewish intellectuals of the Workers Party who had opposed the war now suffered from having sided with those who made no opposition to the Holocaust. The Workers Party drifted towards the right. Max Shachtman himself ended up in his later life committed to the defence of the American state against the subversives of the left, even supporting the American action in the Vietnam War.

By 1947 the Johnson-Forest Tendency was ready to rejoin the Socialist Workers Party. James's political life consisted of studying in depth the works of Marx and Hegel, and working at the enormous task of bringing their complex, recondite ideas to the understanding of the voter, the cinema-goer, the sharecropper, the 'worker', in pamphlets and essays published by the Party. That at least was the ambition. The average voter and the average cinema-goer had never heard of the Party or its pamphlets and was not inclined to be persuaded to try them out.

Yet it seemed to James and the rest of the Party that their formulations were all that stood between the population and the growing

barbarism of the capitalist state. The war had crystallized James's
ideas about fascism. In a pamphlet entitled *The Invading Socialist
Society*, published by the Johnson-Forest Tendency in New York in
1947, he contended that the battle between 'socialism' and 'barbarism' had been joined; that the inner contradiction of the process
of capitalist production had now, universally, as the half-century approached, come to maturity. The workers of the world were manifesting their restlessness in everything they did. To keep capitalism
alive the state intervened in the severest fashion to curtail all revolt.
That was C.L.R.'s definition of fascism.

In 1950, together with Dunayevskaya and Grace Lee, James published *State Capitalism and World Revolution,* a final denunciation
of Stalinism in pamphlet form. It was also James's final break with
Trotskyism of all sorts. Apart from representing Russian socialism
as a brutal form of capitalist organization, James and his collaborators were, for the first time, asserting that the American working
class was revolutionary by instinct and in its self-organization, a
proposition that was shocking at the time and remains dubious
to this day. Their argument was that what held the American working class back was the timidity of its leadership, and its tendency to
sell out.

This may sound like wishful thinking, but it was a line that
James maintained for the rest of his life, never succumbing to the
pessimism of other left-wingers like Herbert Marcuse who went on
to believe that the American worker had been bought by Mammon.
For James, the American workers remained on the side of the angels
but rarely won prizes for harp-playing.

Throughout this post-war period, James was working on his interpretation of the actions of people through the theories of Hegel,
an attempt to use the philosophical method of Hegel to capture the
essence of the Russian Revolution. The typed and cyclostyled version of the book, completed in 1948, was issued to his circle and the
wider Marxising movement as *Notes on Dialectics*. It was not formally published as a book until thirty or so years later in London.
James said he wrote the book because he found in Hegel's theories

the 'algebra' of historical analysis, and for him mastering that was the holy grail of understanding the future in the present.

How James, Lee and Dunayevskaya came together in these collaborations is even now a matter of contention. From the evidence of the letters that flowed between them, it seemed that the collaboration was carried on by correspondence. James would direct studies, each of them being given a task which they were to fulfil and then invite criticism from the others. The process was democratic in the extreme and self-protective. James wrote: 'Within this circle I can polemicize against Grace. One step out of it and I wouldn't.'

It was at this time, in the months in which the book on dialectics was being formulated, that James met Selma Weinstein, a young Jewish recruit of the Correspondence Group, who would later follow him to England and become his third wife.

The Johnson-Forest Tendency ended sadly, in an episode which illustrates how illusory and petty was the world in which these would-be architects of world revolution lived.

'Freddie Forest', really Raya Dunayevskaya, being Russian herself, speaking the language and reading the texts in the original, always felt she had a better grasp of European matters than James, the black man, the ex-colonial who shared a radical platform with her. He didn't read German and he didn't read Russian, but when he was confronted with a word like *aufhebung* in the works of Marx or anyone else, he would chase it like hounds after a fox or a surgeon after an irregular heartbeat.

The disagreement was over the writing of *Notes on Dialectics*. As part of the process, it was Johnson's task to read Hegel's *Philosophy of Mind* and to report back on it. Freddie Forest considered that Johnson had failed to grasp Hegel's ideas, whereas she understood them. She would quote, over and again for years after, Johnson's assertion in a letter to Grace Lee that he 'had looked at Hegel's *Philosophy of Mind* and got nothing from it'. The implication was that it was Freddie who really formulated *Notes on Dialectics,* or at least the passages that make sense. C.L.R., however, published *Notes* under his name alone.

As late as 1991, after Johnson's death, a collaborator of Freddie's called Lou Turner, presented a paper at a conference entitled 'C.L.R. James: His Intellectual Legacies' and repeated the story that Freddie had been peddling about James 'getting nothing' from *Philosophy of Mind*. But in 1997 Aldon Lynn Nielsen, in *C.L.R. James: A Critical Introduction*[8], with access to the microfilmed letters of Johnson and Lee, quoted the actual lines: 'I have not been doing much but I went over Mat'm and Empirico-C [sic: he means Lenin's Materialism and Empirico Criticism]; and had a good look at the *Philosophy of Mind*. I got nothing from the second—for our task now, but I have a hunch something is there for us.'

The dispute which caused the split rankled for forty years.

In a statement which is included in the second cyclostyled version of the *Notes on Dialectics*, James wrote: 'I come to the United States and have to take up dialectic. I am no philosopher. That was a job for a trained academic who had embraced Bolshevism. Luckily *Grace Lee* [author's italics] was there to help . . .'

The disclaimer was disingenuous. He had for ten years been studying Marx and had now resolved to go back to Marx's framework of thought, which he believed was to be found in Hegel's dialectic. *Notes on Dialectics* is, however, a strange book. It tries to introduce the reader to Hegel without telling the reader what Hegel said. Hegel was a German etymologist, a philosopher who challenged Kant's notion that a mind sees the world, that the mind is subject and world is object. Hegel put forward the attractive thought that the mind cannot formulate a concept without seeing its negation. That sounds very difficult but becomes easy when one thinks of the coastline on a map. If this is land, the stuff beyond the line is not-land, or sea in this instance. The mind apprehending the boundaries of a concept must see in the defining instance, the borders, the outsides, that which doesn't belong to the concept. This is a development of Plato's ideas of the mind's apprehensive methods. Marx seized on Hegel and declared the end of philosophy for rhetorical, rather than academic purposes.

James, and Grace Lee, took Marx literally and, ignoring the arguments about how the human mind apprehends, proceeded to formulate three rather simplistic themes. Firstly, they claimed that 'the dialectic' as formulated by Hegel meant that everything turns into its opposite. Hegel's work says no such thing. The second idea espoused by James and Lee was that an entity, be it an institution or an idea, has within the concept of it, its own seeds of conflict and destruction. This may not apply to an entity like 'sky' but applies to an entity like 'capitalism' within which there are workers who will be dissatisfied and make moves to destroy it. This was not a new or startling theory.

The third idea that emerged from the book was that of social organization. But it wasn't Hegel who wrote specifically of social institutions; it was Marx. James and companions floated the idea of 'universals'. By this they meant formations of people to carry forward the fight against capitalism. The first such 'universal' according to them was the Paris Commune of 1871 when for a few weeks the workers of Paris ran their own government of the city and promulgated some wide and liberal edicts. Marx himself said, 'The Commune was in no way socialist, nor could it be', and yet it was chosen as an exemplary historical moment by James and his colleagues because it stated that among the objectives it never had the time to achieve was free education and a fixed working day for a fixed wage. The Commune was overthrown after bloody fighting by the French Assembly whose army had retreated to Versailles and returned to reclaim the capital from the Communards.

The next 'universal' was the collections of workers and soldiers in Russia called the Soviets. They joined the Party of the revolution and that Party triumphed and as the dialectic predicted (according to James *et al.*) turned into its opposite.

In later years, after the Hungarian revolution of 1956 and the Polish revolt of *Solidarnosc* (Solidarity) in the 1980s, James claimed that *Notes on Dialectics* had pointed towards a new 'universal': the workers' committees that would destroy the Soviet Union, a historical collapse whose beginnings he lived to see.

The *Notes on Dialectics* do not make good reading. They were not written in the coherent prose characteristic of James's other work. It almost seems as if James leaned to the obscurantism of the academics in order to prove that he, animated by proletarian zeal, was better than they were.

In one sense, the book was James's way of working out what he really wanted to say about the transformation of societies. His reading in Marxism had been most thorough; his understanding of America, of popular culture, the most advanced; his renunciation of leadership through a party and his denial of the prescribed Leninist role of this party in modern times, a unique progression.

James was always a great explainer and, throughout his life, possibly from the time he began to teach at Queen's Royal College, he took the most complex subjects and made them simple. He was always able to summarize the essence of a painting or a book. I remember only one other occasion when he failed to illuminate something for me, and that was his attempt to introduce me to the final quintets of Beethoven. He would sit me down next to his bed and ask me to put the records on. When I didn't share his enthusiasm, he was disappointed. James's response to my lack of enthusiasm was to tell me they would appeal if I listened to them again and again, as I grew older. It was an uncharacteristic response and he refused to explain it.

There are for me other puzzles in James's life as a critic. His work on Melville and Shakespeare, his comments on the English poets and on American writers are to me crystal clear and original. The one central obscurity in his literary critical *œuvre* was his espousal of the work of a Guyanese novelist named Wilson Harris. He urged me to read him. I tried but could make head nor tail of the stories nor indeed of the sentences. James put this down to my ignorance, insisting that it was fine writing. He declined to explain the bits I read out to him. Harris's sentences are opaque constructions which

I firmly believe James himself didn't penetrate. Yet he insisted on the excellence of the prose as embodying the philosophy of the German existentialists Martin Heidegger and Karl Jaspers. There is no evidence in Harris's novels of either influence, but James wanted there to be.

Deep insight or fraud? I would ask myself this as I turned off his lights and set the alarm for six-thirty when he would wake up and demand his precisely boiled, three-and-a-half minute egg.

James was deported from the USA in what was later known as the McCarthy era. He spent his last few months there in detention on Ellis Island and then was given his passport and sent by ship to Britain. His judgement on the McCarthy phenomenon, writing in the sixties, is that Senator Joseph McCarthy was sponsored by factions of the ruling establishment of America to terrorize and warn the working-class movement into obedience. The bogey of the communist sympathizer and subversive within the media and the organizations of the working class was set loose, but James was of the opinion that McCarthy failed in this aim. Some actors and writers in Hollywood were blacklisted and some trades union leaders indicted, but the working-class movement of America, being nebulous and not being under the control of a communist party, escaped the intended consequences.

5

Through the Looking Glass

The boat is small but riding as in a bath. The sun is as hot as fire, in a bluish-green, blue and white sky. The revolutionary can't pronounce the boat's name, which is *Tegucigalpa*. He says he has only twelve words of Spanish. He has made friends on board with a Mexican tenor who, conversely, can speak only ten words of English. The tenor is heading for Rio de Janeiro for his first public booking. He tells the revolutionary that, when they stop in New Orleans, he must help him buy tails. Music bridges the language barrier.

At breakfast, the tenor and the revolutionary sing together. The revolutionary, from his cultured life in Trinidad and his sophisticated sojourn of seven years in England, has memorized some arias. He doesn't speak Italian and his German is elementary. But he has taught himself a little French and, with the help of a young lady in Normandy, he once translated a voluminous work of the political history of the Soviet Union into English.

The revolutionary is thirty-eight years old. He is on his way back from Mexico where he has had talks with Trotsky. On the boat, apart from singing and stealing the precious hot bath water that the tenor has run for himself, he interrogates the negro sailors and cooks. He finds that he needs to teach them nothing by way of agitation about their wages, the company's profits, the tax evasion of the boat company that has registered the vessel in Honduras, or anything else about their world of work and their relationship to it.

Our story is set in 1939, in the months just before the Second World War and New Orleans still practises segregation on the buses and in its taxis. The revolutionary has been warned about the South. On landing he will have to phone for a taxi that accepts blacks and not try to pick one up as white passengers do. All this and more he explains in a letter to a young lady he has met a few days previously.

When he arrived from England on a six-month visa to begin his lecture tour as a guest member of the Fourth International, the revolutionary was introduced to this young lady. He was also introduced to her husband, who was a member of the Party, and to her brother-in-law and others, all aspiring revolutionaries.

In later letters, he is to tell this young lady, who is called Constance, that he noticed her from the platform as he spoke. And more so when she asked him a question at the end of the speech.

Constance was quite taken with him too. A sophisticated Negro speaking fluently and without notes, a born orator, or one who appeared to the manner born, was unusual, unique, in her experience.

Her first impression of him was one of fascination. She writes years later that he struck her as a magnificent and sleek racehorse, with his long neck craned forward. He seemed as trained and tuned to speak as athletes are to run and jump.

Her appreciation of his particularity as a speaker is acute. She says that he voiced the half-submerged ideas of his audience and this was his great skill. He also made them feel part of something larger than that hall: 'Here was the broad, wide world of imagination and heart. Here was an international movement.'[1]

After the meeting, Mrs Marcus Garvey, the wife of the enigmatic leader of the Back to Africa movement, had approached the revolutionary. 'You don't act like a black man,' she had said and everyone knew what she meant.

The revolutionary prides himself on being able to sum up tensions between people. Looks, gestures, a few words suffice. The revolutionary has specially cultivated this gift of observation. Between Constance and her husband he senses such a tension. He sees something and surmises the rest.

Who is she? She is a young, white Los Angeles student revolutionary who very much wants to be part of the fight against American injustice, wants to be part of the movement that supports and nurtures the oppressed, part of something international, part of history. She also wants to be an actress and later, much later, tells him that she wants to be a poet.

She is only eighteen when their first meeting takes place. She is tall with penetrating, dreamy eyes and hair in a forties wave. Her family is from the South, from Atlanta, Georgia. The 'black question' which begins with unease about poverty and a collective guilt, occupies her. It seems that no one in America can cauterize the wound, solve the problem, assuage the guilt or shift the responsibility.

Christian cults blame the devil and say sorry. There is atonement, exoneration at a stroke. But still the churches remain segregated. The socialists analyse the guilt away and offer absolution in the form of blaming another devil—the nascent capitalism which enslaved Africans and dragged them to the new world. With them, redemption is to be found through the Party and working for the overthrow of the corrupt legacy.

At their first meeting, Constance Webb is impressed. The revolutionary goes on to impress her further by writing to her constantly as he travels.

Here the revolutionary is, with a marriage that remains buried in a past he has put behind him, returning from his talks with Trotsky, with plans to transform the not-happening American revolution. There have been other rooms, other questions. What does he want from her?

In all his first letters he asks her to write to this or that port, poste restante. She replies to only one in five of these letters.

The revolutionary goes back to his cabin and finishes one of his long letters to this Constance. He is literary, witty, he tells her a story he has remembered from his Trinidadian background. He constantly says how much he wishes she was with him, as though they had been lovers for years. He writes flirtatious phrases and then doesn't post the letters.

He sends her shorter letters, ones with a few of the same elements, but without the long descriptions of the sea cruise. Later on, when he has gathered confidence, when there is no going back on their commitment, he will ask her permission to send these unsent letter as proof of the kind of attention he wanted to pay her from the beginning.

The revolutionary begins to think of the enormity of the tasks he has ahead—changing the world, changing morality by challenging the conditions that inform it, intervening in history.

It fills him with a sense of the unreal. He feels the need of another world into which he can escape. It is as though Alice had charge of the elixir that took her into Wonderland and, if she can't go through the looking glass, she can at least write to the White Rabbit every day.

This is the question: what is the revolutionary doing writing these letters to an eighteen-year-old when he himself is nearly forty? This is the answer: he is finding himself. The revolutionary is not the type to confess to a diary. If he keeps a diary at all, it must immediately be its opposite. It must have a public and dramatic purpose.

His purpose deepens as he writes and she responds. It doesn't matter that for years he isn't in the same town, doesn't see her, doesn't kiss her, doesn't know any more about her than what she chooses to reveal and what mutual friends, unaware, report.

He has no one else to whom he can confess this compulsion of his being, the criticism of plays, the day-to-day life of his mind, by which he is intrigued; he needs to cultivate a relationship in which nuances, compared to the great ambitions of revolution, are not seen as trivial. In these letters—subtle at all times, self-conscious to the point of pain, restrained, strategic, effusive in their expression of his own thoughts and generous in his attention to any detail of her life she cares to interpose in her replies—the revolutionary is living a double life.

Although he is too keen an observer of character not to know the real person and her frailties, he constructs this person to whom he is writing. He has gauged, from a very few meetings in company, never by themselves, what this girl is about. He is subtle enough never to boast to her about this particular predictability. He can be insightful, penetrating, even withering about the construct of other people's characters, but not of hers. In fact, he is wooing her.

He is torn between treating her as a pupil and treating her as an equal who can return his love. He fills his letters with disclaimers—she must not think he is patronizing her, but he urges her to read this and that and constantly instructs her.

He writes to her about plays and poetry and music. He sends her profound critical thoughts which could have been refined and expanded into articles for the European literary or artistic press. The journals which the revolutionary writes for in America are not particularly interested in 'bourgeois poetry', or in D. H. Lawrence's writings about love. These he must try out on Constance in Neverland. On himself.

He tells her about his past love affairs. He says he understands her situation because he had a Dutch girlfriend in Britain, a married woman of fine stature and sensibilities who was married to a rich man.

Like a smitten schoolboy, he asks Constance for photographs and tells her how much she is in his thoughts. For years he proposes nothing, but the words he uses are intimate—'sweetheart' and 'my dearest Constance'. He frequently plays the valiant knight in his letters, the game of 'command me and I shall fly to your side'.

But still they are apart. She tells him of her life and loves only when these begin to overwhelm her and he gives her advice, sometimes profound advice, to break loose, to find herself, to have faith in her abilities. About his own political meandering he says very little.

Now and then he boasts about the audiences he has impressed or the fine articles he has written. When he pours scorn on the Communist Party and its positions and activities, his remarks are animated partly by the fact that he knows Constance has fallen in love with an actor, Jack Gilford, who is a communist sympathizer.

Constance goes through three relationships during the first five years of the ten-year correspondence. She writes, when she is so inclined, to the revolutionary about these affairs and he gives her advice in which there is no sense of hurt or jealousy. He mentions nothing of any relationships he may have formed.

He is different from other men. He will not repress the artistic woman: 'I want a woman who is a personality in her own right—the more powerful the better. The more removed from my own field, the better I can stand up to her. I am not afraid.'

Thus begins the second act of the drama.

The revolutionary has constructed the perfect woman in the correspondence. She is now free to be his. And he sets out to claim her.

His allusions to Romantic poetry, his quoting and explaining Keats and Byron, would in themselves win over the hearts of hundreds of young women, but he compounds these with a flattery of her own verses which he demands and she hesitantly sends.

The letters tell their story. They are not testimony to the clichéd tension or 'contradiction', as the cultists call it, between the personal bourgeois life and the revolutionary duty. There is from the start a dishonesty of perception. The young Constance has her own life to live. Her avowed admiration for the Negro speaker is not going to get her seriously to devote her life to studying three volumes of Marx with him. He wants her to follow him into Hegel, into Hemingway and Faulkner. She will read D. H. Lawrence when he is being denounced by the female comrades and she will come to an understanding of the quality of love which the revolutionary finds uniquely described there.

She will read the Greek plays and Shakespeare and learn from him the real meaning of *Hamlet* and the difficulties he has with Paul Robeson's static, uncomprehending portrayal of Othello. She will read Keats and Eliot and Yeats's essay on poetics just to share his enthusiasms and approvals.

And, of course, she does nothing of the sort. She carries on with her life of acting bit parts, trying to be a model, making love to her succession of partners and writing poetry.

The revolutionary, sensitive to a historical sweep of poesy, making stunningly confident and interesting judgements about poetry in the English and American traditions, tolerates and praises her verse:

> *But I am not returning*
> *I shall grow*
> *You saw lace edge and*
> *too late feel relentless*
> *blue*
> *I cannot be silent*
> *I am not afraid*
> *and out of me shall*
> *return*
> *A new life*
> *I defend you because*
> *You are my life*
> *I perhaps gave you*
> *up to-day . . .*
> *But I gave you up*
> *I see the path . . .*
> *and see it is mine*
> *the path I must follow*
> *my feet follow*
> *Their pointing . . .*
> *My life is no longer*
> *Mine*
> *I gave it . . .*
> *Though my love*
> *Asks not*
> *My returning*

I cannot go . . .
I must not return . . .
I must remain alone.

He says, 'you . . . show a tremendous advance and show real power. Language, images, sense of structure, dramatic contrast are stimulated by the conflict . . .' Does he believe a word of it?

He goes further. Writing to her of Keats and Shelley, he says: 'for my part, to-day, without seeing another line if you decided to make writing your main, your only purpose in life, I personally would stake my reputation on your ultimate success'.[2]

He does not tell her how he lives, how he makes his money or any other detail of his practical life. It's true he once or twice alludes to himself furnishing a room or doing the shopping, but even in this he is playing the little-boy-philosopher hybrid who will awaken her motherly instincts.

Finally, not through the revolutionary's persuasiveness, but because there is a job on the New York stage, Constance Webb comes East.

The revolutionary and Constance meet once again, face to face. They live together for a very short time. Despite this, his side of the correspondence doesn't stop. He is still writing to her. The diary won't dry up simply because the needs of distance are no longer there.

While they are together, he gets a divorce from the first wife he left behind in Trinidad. It is a troublesome divorce. He can't risk exposing his presence to the authorities because he has outlived his visa. He must do the deed by letter, getting a decree from the divorce factory of Reno. The revolutionary then returns to the East and proposes to Constance who, after his constant entreaties and being isolated in New York, agrees. They marry and have a child.

Left-wing factions don't pay wages to writers and activists. The leaders among them rely on donations from rich or working sympathizers and the revolutionary has earned small sums of money from his writing for market publishers and has sustained himself through the patronage of political disciples who lend him apartments and keep him in food, clothes and books.

Now he needs a proper job. The factionalism of the movements and 'tendencies' of which he has been a part has subdivided his following and the separate parts make no sort of lucrative whole. The Johnson-Forest Tendency itself breaks up into Johnson and Forest and if it were possible, and if they had persisted, no doubt the Forest would split into its individual dissenting trees and John and his Son would eventually be parted.

He prepares to write a book on American civilization, for which he can get an advance from a bourgeois publisher. He goes to the farm of James Drackert, a friend, and begins work. He has left Constance in New York. His son is about to be born. He has quarrelled with Constance just before he set out and writes to her now to patch it up. The quarrel doesn't get much mention. He doesn't understand their incompatibility and never will. He writes what he knows, saying that everyone has a little bit of the *petit bourgeois* in him and that she should fight herself and this demonic 'other' which breeds ambitions inconsistent with the life and duty of a revolutionary.

Their son, C.L.R. James, Jun., known as Nobby, is born. For the sake of the child perhaps, Constance is reconciled to James and they live together again for a while in New York. But the amity doesn't last. The strains cause her to leave again after a few months. Again he writes to her. He wants her back.

Mentor becomes lover, husband and father. Very soon the impossibility of integrating the world of the correspondence, the imagined world of a harmonious developing, mature relationship, with the world in which the revolutionary lives, becomes evident.

There is more in evidence. There are the *petit bourgeois* demons from which Constance's ambition has not escaped. The revolutionary has to face the stark fact that perhaps these *petit bourgeois* demons are not vestiges of an old lure that Constance has felt, but the personality of the real woman to whom he has been writing.

The story is violent in conclusion. Gone are the boasts of mastering 'the dialectic'. The correspondence now bursts into a stream of consciousness. These notes, written in crisis, possibly at the most painful moment of realization, have no pretence to 'dialectic' or anything else. They are pure, defenceless pain. The revolutionary is not having a breakdown in the conventional sense, but this break and crisis of realization have reduced him to a gibbering idiot.

The part of his life that belongs to Johnson-Forest is troubled, but safe. The part that has been construed by himself in the letters is in tatters.

Here are the 'notes' reproduced as he wrote them in longhand, intending to use them as jottings to guide him through a meeting with Constance after she, inevitably, leaves him. In part the notes are begging her for a meeting. He jots down his intention to tell her how much he loves her and how his love is unique. He rehearses their history, but for the most part it is a cry from the heart, a meandering stream of consciousness, the closest he has come to a breakdown.

The notes begin in confession, though this was probably not how he intended to begin his address.

'*Terrified I was too old for you. You cried when we slept together.*'

And then he anticipates what he suspects is the reason for their breakup. He is going to protest his innocence of any two-timing.

'*Relaxing with women never doing anything else.*'

The quarrel had taken him by surprise. She '*came like a storm . . . battered me I was frightened*'.

His notes touch briefly upon sex, on what they liked doing together and their past sex lives and he asks if they can go over his letters to her '*one by one*'. That should restore her admiration for him.

It is indicative of the fact that the woman he knows and wants back is the one to whom he writes, not the flesh and blood one who fights and behaves in this perplexing way by leaving him.

He wants to tell her that she represents things in his life that his political activity deprived him of, but what nags him constantly as he formulates these notes is the thought that she has gone off with her ex-lover, an actor and a communist. He is going to remind her that this is not merely a matter of ideological differences.

For the only time in his life a new James emerges, one who admits to having lost himself:

> *'Then immediately we married it started*
> *   problem I was nobody I was nothing . . . that's what you*
> *did to me.'*

Then he returns to her lover:

> *'(You are thirty years beyond him).*
> *If you hurt him if he cracks up for a bit. What does it matter?*
> *He will find someone.'*

Then he lapses into bathos. He was badly beaten as a child. He never trusted women. Now the immigration authorities are after him. He needs her for that practical reason:

> *'The marriage will come up and I will say my wife is challenging the marriage. They will say get out. I'll have to go. You are my chance.'*

The notes read as though a second piece of paper with the rest of the sentences, set out to the right of the fragment we have, has been lost, a vertical strip torn and forever gone. But that's not the case. These are the notes the revolutionary made in order to provide some focus and flow for a conversation with his wife.

They are disturbed notes, but through the ramblings emerge the confessions and several secrets. After a bitter quarrel Constance has threatened to return to Jack and to Stalinism. This is a double betrayal.

James feels that the entire process of educating Constance has gone wrong if she can even contemplate a return to the Communist Party or go back to a relationship with someone who is a communist.

The quarrel has been precipitated by Constance's discovery of an affair between Grace and the revolutionary, something which was the subject of gossip amongst his immediate circle but hadn't reached her ears. Grace is, of course, Grace Lee, the Chinese-American Ph.D. from Bryn Mawr, daughter of a rich restaurateur, who joined the left movement and then the Johnson-Forest Tendency as a 'pupil' of the revolutionary (or so he regarded her). In all his letters to Constance, the revolutionary alludes to Grace only once. This is surprising as she is his extremely close associate in the day-to-day business of pamphleteering and political formulation. His reticence on this score covers a deeper friendship than he wants to admit to Constance, or to be questioned about by her. Even here the mention is ambivalent and emerges as a flash in the instant lightning of pain.

The revolutionary also rehearses the list of lovers Constance has had while they consolidated their correspondence and it demonstrates that she was far from committed all that while to his way of thinking. The evidence points the opposite way. She was making love to Jack Gilford and presumably not accusing him of intellectual complicity in the murder of Ukrainian children in concentration camps or the prosecution and execution of Trotsky while she did it.

The revolutionary has figured it out by now. She never did belong to him as he had assumed from his Herculean effort of intellectual seduction.

In this confessional mode the revolutionary is saying, or letting it slip, that he will give up the life of the caucus, of comings and goings and busy political resolutions late into the night in some rented flat paid for by patronage. He seems to be offering on the one hand the bourgeois alternative—just you and me and kids—a bourgeois life with a revolutionary cultural consciousness as the excuse or escape, and on the other saying he will induce her into the caucus.

She can finally be accepted. He had hung back from using his influence to bring his wife into the inner circle. She used to have to retire to the other room when the comrades were in full flow and making up their minds about recommending or rejecting the Second World War on behalf of the American workers. No longer. Now he'll abandon these scruples. She can be part of the caucus. She can stay for the discussion. Even at this stage, where she threatens to abandon him altogether, he doesn't realize that this admission to an inner circle of revolutionary service is not what she is longing for.

Within this freewheeling nightmare of fragments, somewhere the revolutionary confesses that he has constructed the Constance he loves an 1 writes to.

> '*I wanted you to give me what the movement lacked. I tried to keep you from being a political drudge. Perhaps I used this . . .*
>
> *Now it is dead. It is we who made you. Those few who stand for something . . .'*

Women have been told this before and since. The great thinkers, the sacrifices in the cause, standing for something, have made them what they are. It's cult talk. Constance is not falling for it.

A year after their marriage in the summer of 1946 it is not simply on the rocks; the rocks have become the hard place and the hell in which the revolutionary finds himself.

The correspondence continues, with the revolutionary pressing now in clear prose the propositions of his outburst. He asks her to come back. He again makes the offer of a bourgeois life. He recognizes that his rival for her allegiance is offering her just that and the years of trying to instruct and mould her in real Marxism and the real aesthetic have failed. She is her own woman and not a Johnsonian or a Forestian.

The problems with Constance come just after Raya Dunayevskaya and the revolutionary form the Correspondence Group and break away once more from the Socialist Workers Party. This Group in turn breaks up after the revolutionary is deported and a fight breaks out within it about the bill for publishing his latest work on Herman Melville.

Years later, in December 1962, in a letter to his friend and comrade from the 1940s, Martin Glaberman the revolutionary says: 'Even now when I think of it, the work that I used to do, I feel distressed. It is perhaps the only thing in my life which I look back on not so much with bitterness, but with regret, with recognition of the fact that I wasted my strength, my time and my physical health on something that was absolutely useless.'

The revolutionary extricates himself from this absolute uselessness, even though he doesn't feel it at the time, by chance.

The immigration authorities arrest the revolutionary in 1952. There has been a campaign in the newspapers against illegal aliens. The FBI has known about the revolutionary, his whereabouts, his contacts and his writings, but they haven't seen him as a dangerous subversive. They have passed the papers on to the immigration bureau which carries out the arrests and charges the revolutionary with overstaying his visa. The revolutionary counters by applying for US citizenship on the grounds of having been resident there for a long time and having a wife and child who are American citizens. He is sent to Ellis Island for six months while the application is considered.

The revolutionary is in touch with the National Association for the Advancement of Colored People (NAACP), many of whose leaders are intimate friends. He has lectured to the organization and now the organization, large in numbers and with considerable political clout, supports his application.

The revolutionary writes a letter to Walter White of the NAACP which states that the case for refusing him citizenship rests on the authority's contention that *World Revolution,* a book written by the revolutionary, is a subversive document. The revolutionary offers in his letter to destroy every copy of the book since he no longer believes in its premises and arguments. He expects Walter White to intercede with the authorities and say as much to them: the James they've detained is a changed man.

This line of defence is somewhat disingenuous and relies on the fact that the immigration authorities and the judges considering his case will not be smart enough to see that his denial of Trotskyism is not a step back to capitalism.

Years later, in the eighties, while he lived in London, I accompanied the revolutionary to the American embassy in Grosvenor Square to apply for a visa. We stood in the queue outside and wound our way up the steps and in to the desk. America seemed to be a popular destination.

He wore a wide-brimmed hat like a Texas oilman, a dark blue suit and he carried a walking stick. When he took his hat off he had a rich shock of white hair, well barbered. When we got to the head of the queue and he presented his passport, the attendant at the desk excused herself and went into an inner office. Some moments later, a consulate official emerged. He pronounced the revolutionary's name and invited us to go with him.

'Cricket,' he said as we followed him. 'I have read your stuff. I'm unusual. I'm an American mad about cricket.'

In the inner office, we were politely, even effusively, seated. The consular official was pleased that the day had brought some novelty. The files were brought and perused.

'It says here that you were expelled. Ellis Island?'

'That was a long time ago.'

'And everything has changed?'

'A lot has changed. I can tell you I don't believe the things that I used to believe. And I have been in and out lecturing since, but you fellers make me apply each time, so here I am.'

'I am sure there'll be no problem, sir, but I have to check with Washington. Can you leave me a phone number and pick up the visa tomorrow?'

The revolutionary looked at me with a gesture of staged resignation. I said I'd collect it.

There was no problem. The visa was granted.

In fact, James had been back to the States in the seventies but there was no record at the American consulate of his having done so. He had visited Canada and lectured there just before. Had he smuggled himself across the open Canadian border without a US visa? I asked him. He smiled and shook his head.

'Revolution throws me out. Cricket gets me in,' he said.

It has been said that *Mariners, Renegades and Castaways* was written as part of his plea to remain in the United States. If so, it is a very strange plea. It certainly claims in its Afterword that Soviet Russia is the enemy, which would perhaps have pleased some patriotic American official. But it also restates the Marxist conviction that capitalism, as represented by America itself, is doomed. Hardly a reassuring formula for demanding continuing residence.

6

A Big White Whale

James's lifelong preoccupation with Shakespeare was matched only by his passion for Herman Melville. For James, Shakespeare was the exemplar of process, of the birth of ideas in an age of uncertainty, when the question 'What is to be done?' is preceded by 'What is to be thought?' and followed by 'Who then is to do it?'

In Herman Melville, and in *Moby Dick* in particular, James found the great allegory for America itself, for the reign of capitalism in its final stage of totalitarian obsession. Moby Dick is Captain Ahab's obsession, the one for which he will sacrifice himself and his crew. For James this represented the quintessence of the allegorical truth about capitalism. Captain Ahab is the personality that is bound to emerge from its ethics. Ahab has to cajole, control and coerce his crew into the quest for the great white whale, Moby Dick. In this, Ahab is the embodiment of capital. In him the abstract takes on human characteristics. His challenge is to subdue nature or be destroyed by it and with the progress of capitalist progression this means laying waste to it. The crew are cast as the workers of the world, alienated from it and kept at an obedient distance by Ahab.

At the enforced end of his stay in the United States, detained on Ellis Island off the shores of New York and awaiting deportation as an illegal overstayer and undesirable Bolshevik alien, James wrote *Mariners, Renegades and Castaways,* an extended essay on Melville and *Moby Dick.*

James was not the least bit bitter about this expulsion or about the enforced detention. In conversation years later, he recalled it as a busy time, filled productively with writing. I asked him how the warders and the police who took him to and from the island behaved towards him and his reply was that they were diligently polite, doing their job without fear or favour. I admit I had wanted to elicit from him complaint about the American hatred of communists, aliens or black people, but none was forthcoming. James never believed that the average American citizen, warder of Ellis Island or not, was 'brainwashed', 'indoctrinated' or 'ideologically conditioned' to hate leftists or communists. Indeed, the political philosophy which he had come to invent and embrace through his experience in the United States was directly antithetical to any such belief. As far as he was concerned, the warders of Ellis Island were caught in organizational and institutional processes and did their jobs. When conditions were right, some would rebel.

The journey that brought him to these conclusions was long and one that shaped his later thinking. In ideological terms, the steps which James took in his late and post-American essays, may not seem huge to the disinterested observer. As we have seen, when James went to the United States he was a sceptical Trotskyist who believed that a new and international collection of political parties inspired by Trotsky's ideas should and would fight their governments, their ruling classes and their armies and set up variant and free forms of socialist democratic republics throughout the world. When he left the United States in 1953, he had not in so many words renounced Trotskyism, but scepticism had blossomed into an independence of thought.

'Blossomed' is perhaps the wrong word; at that stage it was budding. His intellectual revolt would blossom into a full-blown theory over the following ten years. It was these ten years, through the bitter experience of defeat in the practical politics of the Caribbean, that concluded his education. Only then could he formulate what can be seen now as the Marxism of the future.

How had his time in the USA changed him? James had taken some assumptions with him and, through his experience and with a new concentration and urgency to his reading, these were digested into theory, assimilated into the historical logic of Marxism, the creative conduit of his thought. The inspiration for the transformation came from observation.

First, he noted that there was an anger amongst the Negroes of the United States which could not be channelled through the ideological strategies of communist parties. It was an anger, grown out of the memory of cruelties past, which could not be tamed into step-by-step Trotskyist action dedicated to ultimate world revolution.

Second, he saw that the Party was not a vehicle of democratic transport. There were too many splits, too many plays for position. The concept of the Party itself was perfumed with the rank stink of Stalinism.

Third, he studied Marx and Hegel for the first time. His period of Marxizing in the thirties and forties had been based on guess-work and bravado. James was now using his ability to read in depth gained at Queen's Royal and at his mother's knee, to interpret what Marx and Hegel were actually saying.

Looking at *Mariners, Renegades and Castaways* in the context of his life, it can be seen as a culmination of James's insights into the society of the USA. He realized, before the throngs gathered outside branches of McDonald's in the Third World, that it was a society which was going to influence, if not dictate, the culture of the world.

Seizing on Melville's allegory was for James a literary redemption. His American political project had failed. The agitation for which he had arrived in America fourteen years before had come to nothing. It had no following and no victories—no runs on the board as the cricketing James would have said. What he had acquired was an insight into the relationship between popular culture and what he chose to call the revolutionary urge of cultures and nations.

At the end of this American adventure, James wrote with passion about Melville's allegory:

> Melville is not only the representative writer of industrial civilization. He is the only one that there is. In his great book the division and antagonisms and madnesses of an outworn civilization are mercilessly dissected and cast aside. Nature, technology, the community of men, science and knowledge, literature and ideas are fused into a new humanism, opening a vast expansion of human capacity and human achievement. *Moby Dick* will either be universally burnt or universally known in every language as the first comprehensive statement in literature of the conditions and perspectives for the survival of Western Civilization.[1]

For James, Melville's work, culminating in *Moby Dick,* was a search for the story which would epitomize the relation of man to work, man to man, and man to nature.

James had abandoned the idea that the Marxist project was about the exploitation of workers by bosses who took more than their share. He now believed that Marx had a more fundamental oppression in mind, a grievance that preceded the pillage of one class by another and the inequitable sharing out of dollars and cents.

His reading of Melville precipitated the idea that what the modern man sought was liberation from the alienation that the world of capitalist labour imposed on him and on the isolated Ahabs who governed him with totalitarian authority.

There are in the American academies whole libraries of writings on Melville. Yet *Mariners, Renegades and Castaways* doesn't appear in many bibliographies and is very rarely the work used as a critical starting point by other writers on Melville.

Perhaps this is because it tells us more about James than it does about Melville. Apart from being a unique approach to *Moby Dick*, adding substantially and insightfully to our appreciation of the narrative and the tensions of the relationships, it still stands as the sum of James's American years. It is his text of rejection of the political 'Group', the Party, the Tendency, the organization, the conspiracy, the caucus, the activist. It is an assertion that the revolution he had been chasing, as a mad dog chases its tail, was not simply about sharecroppers' wages but was about the battle against the destructive forces within civilization.

Later in life he would refer to the USA as the country of the future socialism. It remained for him the most fascinating country of all. He was intrigued by its society, its potential and its people. Its people and its daily life provided the clues and the stimulus to formulation. Bourgeois literature provided some of the answers.

7

Out of Joint

James the revolutionary constantly saw his times as the end of one era and the beginning of another. He believed that America and its democracy were to herald the new egalitarian and finally socialist order and he believed that new social structures would bring about a new consciousness, new ways of thinking about the self and society. Shakespeare, he believed, had himself lived in such an age and in several plays had explored the birth of new morals and the new consciousness; this was one of the keys to their endurance as works seminal to our civilization.

James read Shakespeare and discussed it with his literary acquaintances for most of his life, and as early as the 1940s began writing about the plays. The real relevance of these essays to C.L.R.'s own development was that at different stages in his life a different play of Shakespeare would pose a problem or offer its solution which he would use to add authority to an argument.

In one letter to Constance Webb in 1940 James wrote about a production of *Othello* and his disappointment and disapproval of Paul Robeson's performance in it, and he began to elaborate his interpretations of several Shakespearean plays in his letters to her. She was an actress and would be impressed.

It is also clear, however, from the early allusions scattered through

James's letters, through several lectures and essays that he wrote in the sixties, to a lecture he gave on TV in his eighties, that James was searching for the political significance of Shakespeare's plays.

The idea of transition, one order giving place to another, one frame of mind being supplanted by the next, became central to C.L.R.'s thought and teaching and it was this that he also saw in Shakespeare. C.L.R. believed himself to be living in a transitional age between capitalism and socialism, with the old order giving way to the new. He and his associates and disciples read the signs of this transition and interpreted them. Theirs was the task of clarification.

In analysing and writing about Shakespeare, James looked specifically for the political dilemmas of the age. In Hamlet he found a man not so much stultified by the processes of thought but someone who is seeing the world anew. Was James looking into Hamlet to see himself and his own new political certainties and uncertainties? Hamlet is certain of nothing and conducts little experiments and plays tricks to gain this certainty: with the play within the play, with Polonius and, most daringly and obsessively, with Ophelia and his own affections.

James saw Hamlet as the embodiment of the transition between an assured or assumed order where wives loved their husbands and didn't assist in their murders, where a younger brother didn't covet the wife and possessions of the elder. Hamlet has to make sense of the disorder, even to put it right.

James said that Hamlet's attempt to probe and examine all former belief makes him a representative of the new order which is emerging from the disordered feudal world. He embodies the first 'capitalist' consciousness. It is curious that James should see this uncertainty and convoluted moralizing as the first inklings of the capitalist consciousness rather than what we have grown to associate this consciousness with—greed, competition and exploitation.

C.L.R.'s main contention, however, was that Shakespeare, through the histories and the major tragedies, was engaged with one of the great political questions of his time: the question of who should be king. And his insight into Shakespeare and his pursuit of this idea through several plays are a bolster to C.L.R.'s own developing argument, his own question: who should govern?

James's argument towards this end began with *Richard II*. Shakespeare draws the portrait of a weak king, one who deserves to be overthrown by force of arms. Richard is self-obsessed and indulgent, unable to defend himself but self-pitying, surrounding himself with the caterpillars of the commonwealth, the flatterers and courtiers who drain the public purse and, because they are bad companions for kings, must be removed. The man of action Bolingbroke, with the complaint that he was denied justice by this same Richard who was ditheringly unfit to dispense it, takes over the kingdom by force of arms.

The play has been seen since Elizabethan times as a charter for usurpers. Richard's argument relies on his divine right to rule, Bolingbroke's on physical power. James saw the dramatic clash between them as the overthrow of the old dispensation and the establishment of the new.

The same Bolingbroke, having seized the throne from Richard II and crowning himself Henry IV, is, in the next play of the historic sequence, subject to grave doubts about what he has done. Did he do the right thing? Is he damned for displacing an anointed king? The question of who should be king intrudes on his last moments. He speaks to his son Hal:

> *God knows my son,*
> *By what bypaths and indirect crook'd ways*
> *I met this crown; and I myself know well*
> *How troublesome it sat upon my head.*
> *To thee it shall descend with better quiet,*
> *Better opinion, better confirmation;*
> *For all the soil of the achievement goes*
> *With me into the earth.*

Hal proceeds in Shakespeare's history sequence, *Henry IV* Part II
and then in *Henry V*, to become one of Shakespeare's blue-eyed
boys, a national hero untroubled by more than the doubts of a general before battle, leading his troops into danger and possible death.
He loses no sleep over inheriting a throne that was wrested by
force.

James's argument, which one can trace through his letter of 1953
to Jay Leyda, and in the BBC lecture on the play in 1962, progressed to *Macbeth*. In this play Shakespeare moves beyond representing the kingly virtues as a style and a manner, the cloak of
nobility with which Henry V seems endowed, and attempts to present a concrete list of them. What virtues should a king have? It is
this catalogue of virtue which Duncan's son, Malcolm, discusses
with Macduff when he comes to the English court to plead with
him to return to Scotland. Malcolm recites the kingly virtues he
professes not to possess:

> *The king-becoming graces,*
> *As justice, verity, temp'rance, stableness,*
> *Bounty, perseverance, mercy, lowliness,*
> *Devotion, patience, courage, fortitude,*
> *I have no relish of them . . .*

In *Macbeth*, Shakespeare provides us with this cluster of require-
ments. He doesn't care to dramatize each of the qualities. Malcolm
remains someone who has run away. He is not cast in any dramatic
situation which would prove that he possesses these kingly virtues.
He tells Macduff that he doesn't have them and then, when Macduff passes his test of loyalty, reverses his statement and seems im-
modestly to waive the disclaimer. He was only testing him; he will
fight for the throne alongside Macduff. Malcolm becomes king
with the playwright's blessing. Whether he fulfils the promise of the
catalogue we are never told.

James used the play merely to illustrate his argument that Shakespeare was progressively preoccupied with the idea of kingly vir-

tues. For James these were humility, patience, courage and forti-
tude, virtues of the brave proletarian. According to James, Shakespeare then goes on to create a character who embodies all these in
his dramatic person.

In *King Lear,* a monarch divides his kingdom. The question is
posed: who should rule? The king in his dotage has resolved on a
division of the realm on the basis of a test of love which he devises.
The test is in itself so vain that the liars and flatterers can pass it and
truth fails it.

The one character who is singularly more sinned against than sin-
ning is Edgar, driven from his father's love by his bastard brother's
envy. Edgar is pushed to the extremes of existence. He becomes the
lowest of the low, a madman living in a cave, braving the elements,
Poor Tom, the archetype of looped and windowed raggedness. He
meets Lear, driven by his daughters and his own vanity into the symbolic storm.

Around Lear the thunder and lightning rage, but the real storm
to which he is exposed is the poverty and suffering, the sheer vul-
nerability of the poor of which as a king he has taken no notice. To
his Fool, his last companion, he says

> O, I have ta'en
> Too little care of this . . .

He is confronted, in his self-created exile, with the misery that the
poor naked wretches, his former subjects, endure. Poor Tom is the
basest of these sufferers. His food has been frogs, toads and tad-
poles, he has withstood in his nakedness the pelting of the elements.
He has suffered what the lowest in the realm experience. It is the
trial by ordeal through which the drama puts Edgar before finally
proclaiming his right to be king.

According to James this is Shakespeare's last word on the question of kingship. Edgar should inherit the earth, because Edgar has
meekly run the whole gamut of social experience. He has been, as a
fugitive from his brother's plot to kill him, through several disguises

and played many parts. He has seen the world through the eyes of the poorest and most despised and this experience enables him to be the custodian of all he has surveyed, to be king. This, contends James, is Shakespeare's implicit democratic impulse. After *Lear,* this preoccupation with the question of who should rule is abandoned. Shakespeare has settled the question and moves on to other things.

In 1983, while writing the lectures which he was to deliver at weekly intervals for transmission on Channel 4 TV in London, he rehearsed the thesis time and again, adding quotes, asking for the texts, asking me to search for a passage, a snatch of which he recollected. I was to find the scene and the act and place a slip of paper in the page of the Collected Works.

As the preparation for the lecture progressed I tried to introduce the subject of *Coriolanus,* a play in which the tribunes of the people are lampooned, portrayed as rabble-rousers and insensitive, dishonest men whose strength lies in the gullibility and clamour of the mob. I put it to James that in this play Shakespeare seems to support the cause of anti-democratic characters. Our sympathy stays, however grudgingly, with Coriolanus, his wife, his mother and his child, and certainly not with the appointed or elected tribunes of the people.

'They were Stalinists,' said James with a twinkle, amused by his own easy dismissal of the play. It was not to be allowed to enter the political argument. Shakespeare wasn't building an argument, he was writing plays and was to be allowed his inconsistencies.

James was aware that Shakespeare had, in two or three plays, created mobs which could be prevailed upon in one way or another by orators and demagogues to ill-considered, hasty action. *Julius Caesar,* I pointed out to him, is not exactly an advertisement for the rule of the people, by the people, for the people. James dismissed my argument as a misunderstanding of the concerns of the playwright at that time. According to him, *Julius Caesar* isn't primarily about who should rule, but about the abuse of democratic power vested in such a ruler by the consent of the people.

This concept of the spirit of democracy speaking through the appointment of a ruler came late in life to James. In the letter written to Jay Leyda, James emphatically stated that Shakespeare could not conclude *Hamlet, Macbeth* or *Lear* in a satisfactory fashion. In each there is an external intrusion. In *Hamlet* he brings in Fortinbras, in *Macbeth* the forces of England, and in *Lear* the armies of the king of France, to bring about a resolution.

But in the case of *Lear,* the forces of France under Cordelia are defeated and she is imprisoned and executed. In fact, the play resolves itself through the mutual rivalry between the individualists Edmund, Goneril and Regan and through the challenge which Edgar issues to Edmund. Later, James realized that he was wrong about *King Lear.* His subsequent reading was more accurate; Edgar does resolve the play. James first put this argument in 1982 in a letter to the literary critic Frank Kermode following Kermode's broadcast about *Lear* on BBC 2.

In his letter, James wrote of Shakespeare's clear concern with government, curiously enough using Hamlet's famous lines:

> *The time is out of joint. O cursèd spite,*
> *That ever I was born to put it right.*

Actors and directors vary in their readings of those lines, but for James the emphasis falls not on 'cursèd spite' or on the time being out of joint, which Hamlet and the audience take for granted, but on 'born'. 'No one can be "born" to govern,' contended James, 'particularly when the time is out of joint. It is the hereditary responsibility that is in question here.'[1]

In the letter to Kermode, he rehearsed his argument about Edgar playing several different roles in his disguise and learning to be 'pregnant to good pity', the quality of sympathy with the poor and dispossessed which qualifies him to be king.

As a curious postscript to this letter to Kermode, James added: 'P.S. To play Edgar in those terms is a colossal task, none more colossal in our time. I propose Vanessa Redgrave.'

The intention was not mischievous, although it was putting a cat among pigeons to suggest a woman, bringing a feminist argument into casting. It was more, I think, James's unfamiliarity with contemporaneous British actors, notably white male ones of the right age, that made him make the proposal.

Besides, Vanessa Redgrave had made, in the decade before this, several pilgrimages to C.L.R. James's side, fancying herself as a Trotskyist politician in a now defunct group called the Workers' Revolutionary Party. This was a fringe group which attempted to enter the Labour Party and work subversively within it, was expelled and hung about the fringes of fantasy politics for several years before destroying itself in a scandal about paedophilia and young female members. As a leading light of this group, Vanessa Redgrave sought out the inspiration of 'black leaders' in Britain and befriended James, who was undoubtedly flattered by her attentions.

One of the persistent myths thrown up by the Black Power movement and by a particularly pernicious and ignorant stream of 'black studies' was that Shakespeare, being one of the iconic white male figures of literature, was a racist, an anti-semite and various other things. In Britain this reactionary ideology took the form of patois poetry in the sixties and seventies, offered not simply as developments in pop but as political challenges to Shakespeare or Keats.

The idea of 'relevance' was taken up by a section of school teachers and editors who argued for the poets of the English canon to be replaced with the verse of Maya Angelou and with other poets who wrote in West Indian dialects, the Jamaican or Trinidadian patois.

This was a view from which C.L.R. profoundly dissented. To him Shakespeare and Keats stood for the expression of civilizing value, the centre of the cultural endeavour of humanity to which he belonged. An episode from his later life, when he was living in Brixton, illustrates this.

To James's flat in Railton Road, above the offices of the magazine *Race Today*, is invited a young poet from Jamaica called Michael Smith. The editor and the magazine's resident poet, the Jamaican-British Linton Kwesi Johnson, have sponsored him on a reading tour. Mikey, as he is known, wears his hair in Rastafarian locks, crowns it with a woolly hat and a cocky attitude. His immediate contact in *Race Today* is Linton Kwesi Johnson who has set his verse to a form of reggae music and has built himself a substantial popularity and following. Linton has made the acquaintance of, or 'discovered', Michael in Jamaica and raised the money to get the impoverished poet to London. There are plans to make him famous.

The plans succeed. Mikey strikes me as a strange character, polite and full of good humour but with an edge of dramatized menace that proclaims that he is an angry young rebel—a quality calculated and cultivated to impress certain sorts of audiences.

Mikey is presented to C.L.R. James, the eminence at the top of the house. As usual, the old man asks him a hundred questions and through meandering and contradictory answers, builds up a picture of this young poet, born in poverty, scrabbling around for a living in Jamaica, selling postcards to tourists on the beach and making up rhymes. He is induced by a twist of fate into the amateur drama circles of the University of The West Indies' Jamaican campus. He is a born mimic and some of the verse he writes is an accurate satire of the Jamaican mistress who employs and bullies servants. Other poems read like doggerel on the page, but his performance of them is striking.

Linton, with great generosity, arranges for several readings and Mikey goes up and down the country and becomes quite famous. The poetry and music attract the crowds and the crowds attract newspapers. Inevitably the arts establishment hears of this young talent and turns up in the person of an Arts producer of the BBC at

Railton Road, from whence the negotiations for Mikey's appearance on TV will take place.

When the BBC producer finds that he is in the same building as C.L.R. James and that Mikey spends quite a lot of time with him, he wants three for the price of one. He will record as part of the programme a conversation between C.L.R., Linton Kwesi Johnson and Mikey Smith. They will discuss poetry.

The cameras follow Mikey through several of his public performances and they record interviews with him. Then comes the day of the tripartite discussion. It is held in the old man's room with the two young black poets in attendance. They discuss the nature of Jamaican dialect. Mikey adopts the stance of the grass roots man, the illiterate, suffering genius who knows no language but the spontaneous revelations of his verse. One can also see the old man becoming increasingly impatient with the stance, asking him to repeat phrases in plain English. This inhibits the progress of the conversation and gets the cameras to stop and start but doesn't deter C.L.R. who seems determined to extract some clarity from Mikey and refuses to bolster the falsehood he believes him to be creating.

The game is blown wide open when, with a sneer, Mikey alludes to 'Shak-uss-peeree. Or whatever he is called.' A sneer too far. The old man calls him to order.

'Now hold on. I have lived most of my life in the Caribbean, I know Jamaica and Jamaican people and I have never heard Shakespeare's name pronounced like that.'

He refuses to let Mikey wear ignorance on his sleeve as a badge of his rebellion. It's the wrong kind of rebellion. He recommends, on or off camera, I can't remember, though I am present at the interview and stand behind the bright camera lights tripod, that Mikey read some Wordsworth and some Shelley.

Mikey stares defiantly but has been corrected. The last scene of the documentary features Mikey standing in the dawn on Westminster Bridge and rendering Wordsworth's sonnet about the scene in a very moving way.

Mikey makes money from the programme and from the recordings and publication that immediately follow. He stays in London for a while accepting engagements and having sex with the groupies who hang around his poetry readings. For a few weeks, he has nowhere to live, having got into some sort of quarrel with the young women who look after the *Race Today* building and, with their blessing, lands up in my house. He occupies the same room that C.L.R. James had and he stalks around for a lot of the night raiding the bookshelves and acquainting himself with the works of Blake and Tennyson. He is vastly impressed and asks me to explain T. S. Eliot to him. I try. He likes the music of it, the 'strange way of talking' as he calls it. He asks me if Tennyson was a lord or whether that was simply his name.

Then Mikey drifts away. Months later I hear that he has gone back to Jamaica, that he was homesick and lost and couldn't handle England. Six months later I hear that he has gone a bit screwy; he argues with all his friends and is manifesting the symptoms of mental instability.

The last we hear of Mikey is that he goes to the political rally of the Minister of Education. There is political tension in Jamaica and open gang warfare in support of the opposing parties in its parliament. Mikey heckles the Minister and disrupts the meeting. He is watched. On his way home two men corner him in a dark alley and stone him to death.

The news of Mikey's death is relayed to C.L.R. He remembers him as the man who tried to call Shakespeare 'Shak-uss-peeree'. He is thoughtful.

'Jamaica, those islands are savage places, man. If they don't find new ways of killing you they dig up the old ones.'

James tried writing plays himself only twice in his life. The first was the play of *The Black Jacobins*. Even while working on the book, he was turning the material of his research into a play which the Stage

Society of Britain agreed to produce on the condition that Paul
Robeson, who was appearing then in musicals in the West End,
agreed to take the lead role. James had met Robeson, which was
not surprising since the black literary or artistic coterie in Britain
was small, making it unlikely that colonials and exiles could avoid
each other. Robeson accepted the commission and alternated the
roles of Toussaint and Dessalines with James himself.

The play was more of a rhetorical tableau than a romantic history, for, in spite of all his reading of Aeschylus and Shakespeare,
C.L.R. had little dramatic talent. The characters were loaded with
rhetorical and expository speeches which lacked any sense of subtext or dramatic conflict. This is not to say that they were simplistic
or flat; they said what the author intended and had a lot to say, but
their complexity seemed plotted, and lacked spontaneity.

James's second attempt at drama was made when he was eighty
and living in my house in London. One day he asked me to take dictation. Sitting up in bed he wanted to dictate a whole play about
Kwame Nkrumah and I was to write it down. I had already had a
play produced in London and C.L.R. questioned me closely about
the writing and staging of it. It became something of an obsession.
The play was entirely planned out in his head, he said. Pen at the
ready, I sat down to take dictation. Day after day, instead of beginning with the words 'Act One, Scene One' and proceeding to a description of the stage and the set, he would tell me the story of
Nkrumah as he knew it. I would remonstrate. I would remind him
that we were writing a play not a political memoir and it had to have
scenes and its characters had to speak lines. He would think that
over and say yes, he understood, but he wasn't ready for that yet.

Several days later he was ready. I had by now equipped myself
with a tape recorder to preserve my patience and asked him to proceed. He said he wanted to start with the revolt of the Market
Women in Accra—a sort of Dance of the Polovtsian Maidens in the
story of Prince Igor. He began to describe a movement of market
women who defied colonial power and taxation. I interrupted him
again and pointed out that this wasn't a play but a historical essay.

'For God's sake, I'll tell you what went on; you write the damned play,' he said.

He didn't concentrate long enough to tell me where the play should begin, who the characters were and how the action was to proceed. After several weeks of intermittent struggle, the project was declared a failure and abandoned.

8

Home Alone

James didn't leave the United States alone. After the Constance episode, while he was pursuing his political work and writing in New York, he met a young political worker called Selma Weinstein. He had been separated from Constance for less than a year but had formed an attachment to this young woman who had been acting as his amanuensis and political confidante in the months before he was ordered to leave the USA.

Selma, who was instrumental in the formation of the Correspondence Group, joined him in London a few months after his banishment. Selma and C.L.R. set up house together, renting a flat in Hampstead in north London. His son Nobby was left behind with Constance in the United States.

On his return to England he was anxious to resume his relationship with cricket. Since he had left for the United States, he had read about cricket, dreamt about it, kept up with its scores and fortunes, but he hadn't seen a live game. Now he could go to the Oval, watch the county matches on TV and reintroduce himself to the Manchester *Guardian* which once again invited him to write for them.

He started with an article aptly entitled 'Return of the wanderer: comparisons between 1938 and 1953'—the years he had spent in the USA. His survey, exciting for the *aficionado* and technically dense for any lay person, summarized the change as an acceleration in the pace of the game. James noted the 'leg-side slip field' for fast bowlers, a placement of fielders behind the body of the batsman to catch him out as the ball glances off the left edge of his bat. He also noted a new routine: (right-hand) batsmen stepping up to the ball with their left foot, watching the ball carefully rise from the pitch to the bat, and sculpting the intended stroke in a split second.

Then he noted the changes off the field. There were now many more women in the crowds. The journalists were given less space by editors and were as a consequence more flamboyant and attention grabbing. Then there was television.

Throughout the season of 1954, he wrote almost every day for the Manchester *Guardian,* reporting on the Pakistani team's tour of Britain and on the county matches.

During this season, James began work on his autobiography through cricket. The manuscript began life as *Who Only Cricket Know*—from Kipling's lines 'What do they know of England, who only England know?'. It was finally called *Beyond a Boundary,* and was finished and published in 1962.

Even as he planned the book, with enthusiastic if uncomprehending encouragement from Selma, James knew it was a departure from everything he had written in America. He would abandon the preoccupation with the larger themes of world revolution.

The book was his return to Britishness, the return of the colonial who had been brought up with English literature, cricket and puritanism, the three ingredients of British bourgeois life.

More than that, it was an admission that as an American revolutionary he had lost himself, or something essential about himself, that made him a revolutionary and was the prime cause of his concern with world revolution.

Here in Hampstead with Selma, who was an ardent but not uncritical apostle, James set out to reclaim himself from the American years. He would write about himself and his family, about the neighbourhood and the neighbours he had in the country and in Port of Spain in Trinidad. He would write about the divisions of class in the colonial society and the attitudes and snobberies they bred. He would tackle the question of race, so prominent and predominant in the minds of the Americans with whom he had lived and worked and so different in dimension in the experience of the Caribbean colonial.

Above all he would make it a personal book, an autobiographical effort in which one would be constantly aware of the principal character, the observer. It was to be James's return to writing as an artist as opposed to pamphleteer or theoretician.

He was aware as he began that he could not hope to write fiction set in the United States and the places in which he had lived for the last fourteen to fifteen years. He was a great admirer of Richard Wright, and outside the sphere of black writing considered Norman Mailer, whom he met and interviewed before he wrote *The Naked and the Dead,* above the rising consciousness of the American mass. Besides Wright and Mailer, he considered William Faulkner the finest American novelist of the twentieth century, but he knew that America as fiction was not within his creative grasp. On the other hand, the Caribbean as a subject of contemporaneous fiction had become a remote place to him and Britain was best left to the British writers. No, he would go back to the essential task of mining his memory.

He wrote knowing that his themes—cricket, of which he was a religious disciple, English literature, and puritanism, the creed which he felt still governed his moral thinking, placed him in 'violent contrast with the people among whom [he] had lived'. But he didn't flinch from the potential conflict. He was even inviting it. He had grown tired of the internecine bickering within the shrinking groups of political activists who were in reality his followers.

During the years in which he began the book, he and Selma Weinstein were in touch with the Correspondence Group, writing articles and correcting position papers by post. The paper was, as a consequence called *Correspondence*. The group in turn sent what money they could to help sustain their leader in exile and, as they saw her, his helpmate.

Correspondence was based in Detroit. Its pages, including its dire attempt at cartoons and irony, were testimony to the impossibility of applying James's fine thoughts about culture and Marxism to factory agitation. On the one hand, James was writing with deep insight and perfect literary substantiation about Melville's place in literature and the allegorical nature of his characters. On the other, the Group, whose practice and propaganda were supposed to stem from James, produced plodding, childish material worthy only of high school radicals.

The Correspondence Group finally broke up under the pressure of Raya Dunayevskaya's resentment. She had been James's comrade through thick and thin, through their exits from and re-entrances to the Trotskyist Socialist Workers Party. Now she resented having her strings pulled from across the Atlantic.

The Detroit car workers were at the time being sold several rival radical newspapers. There was the one from James Cannon's Party, then one from Shachtman's breakaway Party, another from the Correspondence Group.

Together James and Dunayevskaya had come to one firm conclusion. This was that the American people were much too sophisticated to be led by a Vanguard Party as Lenin had wanted it to be, a party which would think on behalf of the working class, issue 'lines' and slogans and rules on their behalf.

This was what distinguished the Correspondence Group from the others peddling their ideological line to largely indifferent Detroit workers. With James's deportation, Dunayevskaya, however, while having gone along with the theory in his presence, couldn't see herself functioning without an organization even if it wasn't called the Vanguard Party. She was of the opinion that if you were a revolutionary you had to do something; James's increasingly rigorous point of view seemed to be in favour of doing nothing except observing what the people themselves did and describing its revolutionary potential. From across the Atlantic the debate progressed with Selma and James on one side and Dunayevskaya on the other.

What the conflict boiled down to was, what was the organization of revolutionaries to do? Behind the question was undoubtedly the role of leadership. What position would the ideologues occupy in the revolution? Lenin, Trotsky and even Stalin had, by virtue of their ideology, been leaders and written themselves into history. This evolved Marxism seemed to confine the thinkers of the finest thoughts to at best the position of commentators and editors. James was reconciled to the role. It is apparent that Dunayevskaya, after all the years of supposed evolution of the idea, was not.

Her objection as she stated it, though, was bluntly to demand what the organization should do day to day in the glorious revolution when it came. James was sceptical of her objection. It seemed to indicate that his longstanding philosophical partner had not understood the basis of his fundamental argument. James said in reply that he wanted 'mass democracy'.

To Raya, this meant, in a commonsensical way, changing leaders every week and listening intently and with the same credence to anyone who came along in the name of the people. Any person was 'the people'. One would have to learn to suffer fools gladly and every day the focus one had worked towards would be diffused. It was too much to take.

James either hadn't taken the time to formulate any alternative activity for this organization that would replace the Vanguard Party, or it remained unclear even to him. Now from England he sent the group a new pamphlet, *Every Cook Can Govern*[1], containing his thoughts. The masses of the world must be invited into the Party and into government. James had in mind the example of the Greek city states. He was putting forward the idea of the high political consciousness of ordinary men and women without prescribing a concrete form of government. It would be difficult, however, to see how New York or Los Angeles could be governed by a rotating register of citizens and to the Dunayevskaya sceptics it must have seemed a long shot. Were they really to try and convince the citizens of Detroit or Chicago that they would be called upon in rotation to govern the city, state and country?

In a subtly stated attack on Raya Dunayevskaya's position within Correspondence, James sent the Group an essay on the revolutionary potential of the American working class. In it he says:

> *Correspondence,* I am glad to note does not advocate 'the revolution'. As a rule, small papers which do that usually make themselves ridiculous, and ineffective for what they can really do. No revolution in the world can be made or stimulated by a small newspaper. A small paper which advocates 'the revolution' is usually viewed with scepticism if not amusement by the workers. But any working-class paper has not only the right but the duty to analyze Marxism seriously.

He goes on to say that his socialism is simply defined as the 'organization of production by people who work' and that the aim of a future socialism will be to free humanity from the dehumanizing aspects of work.

In the same essay, 'Marxism and the intellectuals', James says that the solution to the problem is not simply shorter working hours and better wages; it is freedom from the alienation of the work process which means that their capacities as thinking and planning humans are curtailed by mechanical and subservient activity. The disciplines of work have to be converted from the restrictive and the stunting to the liberating and life-enhancing.

There are no prescriptions in the essay, but James is clearly approaching a method of thought, an amalgam of the ideas of popular culture he had acquired and their application to the sterile political formulations he had inherited from the ideological groups.

The essay, however, was refused publication by the Correspondence Group and precipitated his break with it.

Writing from England, it seemed to be James's ideas of popular culture, forged during his period of recuperation in America, which were, for the first time, nudging him towards an answer to the central question, still the one that Lenin asked: 'What is to be done?'. This time Raya was asking it.

James's answer was: nothing is to be done. When people find their lives intolerable they will change them themselves. They will have individuals speak for them, they will throw up administrative leaderships, but nothing, nothing apart from thinking and analysing, can be done to make them change. Years later this idea seemed to be borne out in far off Poland and C.L.R. pointed to it with the rare satisfaction of the prophet.

James was now telling the Correspondence Group to look at popular art through their politically critical training. It was too much for Dunayevskaya. She quit the Correspondence Group and, when she left, she took with her the filing cabinets, the furniture, the books, the typewriters, everything except the unsold piles of old pamphlets and newspapers.

The departure of Dunayevskaya was the final blow. A rump of activists was left in the Correspondence Group but they were advised by Selma and by James not to fight to retain the name of the group. The residual rump began calling itself the Facing Reality Group after a series of lectures and pamphlets which James wrote, with Selma's assistance, to outline the philosophy of the non-Vanguard organization. The group also started to call itself 'Jamesian'.

James sent the first few chapters of the cricketing autobiography to the Facing Reality Group. In a letter to them dated March 1957, he outlined the plan of the entire book, implying that he had already written several chapters of it and issuing an immodest challenge: 'I defy [you] to read those first three chapters without at a certain stage being moved to tears.'

In 1956, James and Selma were married in London.

The book on cricket was not completed for a few years. It was interrupted by an invitation that arrived from the Caribbean, an offer which James and Selma decided they couldn't and shouldn't refuse.

. . .

James realized, through his contact with the new novelists who were emerging from the Caribbean, V. S. Naipaul, George Lamming and Wilson Harris, that his role as a novelist was over. Apart from the cricketing autobiography which he would write with novelistic flair, he set out to write critical essays on popular culture and relate this culture to the political mission he was still conceiving. James was quite aware of the differences between Hamlet Prince of Denmark, and Humphrey, Prince of the Silver Screen. Yet he was convinced that there was a profundity to the response to these forms which may not be present in the forms themselves.

He began writing essays as the first philosopher of trash as art. Since then, whole departments of universities have dedicated themselves to popular culture, by and large for the same reason: if a lot of people love it, let's understand it. The sterile academics of the eighties and nineties, imitators of the convoluted styles of 'deconstruction' who call themselves 'cultural critics', haven't the inspiration or the motive of the native James. He was looking for the revolutionary impulse in popular drama. He didn't find stories in which a million workers raise their fists to the sky and brutally kill capitalists, imperialists, people who wear ties, etc. He wasn't looking for the bathos of Robert Tressell's *The Ragged Trousered Philanthropists* either. What he was looking for and what he did find again altered his definition of what the revolution was and his role in it. But not without interruption. For a year or two the unexpected invitation from the Caribbean, a temptation to start a new life as a practical political activist, albeit in the smaller theatre of Trinidad, tempted him into disastrous misadventure.

When he returned to London after this episode, he resumed the role of cultural critic. At a meeting in London in the 1980s, James advised the assembled black activists he was addressing to 'go and see D. W. Griffith's *The Birth of a Nation*' which was then being shown at an art cinema in Notting Hill. He said he had seen it several times. The film's revival had been featured in the newspapers. Some critics, taking their cue from the fact that it showed the Ku

Klux Klan at their Negro-burning best, objected to it as 'racist'. A bolder member of the audience pointed this out to James who reflected for a moment before replying, 'I would recommend you go and see it in the morning and picket in the afternoon.'

Later, when we were alone, I asked him if this wasn't a cynical response. He was contemptuous of the word. 'Listen, Griffith did pioneering work in cinema. Lenin sent him an invitation, asking him to come and help the Soviet film industry after seeing that very film. What's good for Lenin is good for me, man.'

9

No One Comes to His Party

While he was editing *The Nation*, James was writing his series of lectures, later collected and published as *Modern Politics*. One of the enduring stories of Trinidadian politics is that Dr Eric Williams, having been a professor at Howard University, returned from the United States and gave a series of public lectures in Woodford Square on Greek civilization and other subjects beyond the grasp of the majority of his ecstatically appreciative audience. The lectures, comprehended or not, were the basis for his formation of a political party to oppose colonial dominance. Williams had proved that he was an orator and fit to lead.

It was this example and achievement that James had in mind when he launched his own series of lectures in the central library. The lectures revealed James's general agenda for Trinidad. They were not specifically subversive of the colonial native self-government of Eric Williams which was taking Trinidad and Tobago towards the goal of independence. They are, however, examples of James's oratory at its best: simple statements of what a twentieth-century economy, a twentieth-century working population and the West Indian people can aspire to.

Later, when James had broken with Williams and left the island of his birth, Williams banned the collection from Trinidad. He knew that even while serving him as editor of the Party paper, *The Nation,* James was being subversive and when he had accepted his invitation to join Trinidadian politics he had brought with him his own agenda.

Towards the end, James put his personal stamp on *The Nation,* though he was careful to reflect the views and activities of the People's National Movement, the PNM. James and his staff, who shared his subversive perspective, were waiting for an issue and in 1960 they found one. They used the pages of *The Nation* to run a campaign to award the captaincy of the West Indies cricket team to Frank Worrell, a universally respected black player. The Cricket Board chose the wicketkeeper of the team, F. C. M. Alexander, a white man, to lead the team. James wrote article after article criticizing their choice on the grounds that Worrell would be a better captain and was better qualified as a cricketer.

There was a racial edge to the selection of Alexander. Worrell had stepped in and been granted the captaincy of the team when the West Indies toured India the year before. Now there was an impending tour of Australia and an unstated assumption on the part of the selectors that the West Indies ought to be led by a white man in a white country. James opposed the assumption and admitted in his articles that, though there was a current of racial nationalism in the public support for a Worrell captaincy, his own arguments would leave race out and concentrate on the cricketing prowess of the two players. It was a disingenuous argument, because as C.L.R. acknowledged when discussing the affair in *Beyond a Boundary* which he was writing at the time, implicit in the argument was the racial issue and every reader would pick up on the unstated preference for a white man to lead the team.

The campaign succeeded. Worrell was appointed captain. Worrell wanted to take on his team a Jamaican fast bowler called Roy Gilchrist who had been suspended from the team by the selectors for disobeying the umpires and for general indiscipline during the team's tour of India. James attempted to run a campaign for the reinstatement of Gilchrist. This campaign, which consisted of writing

open letters to the selectors and publishing interviews with eminent citizens which contained testimonies to Gilchrist's good character, brought the political agenda of *The Nation* and C.L.R.'s own
passion for cricket together. He wrote about the reinstatement of
Gilchrist as politically expedient because, as an uneducated rural
Jamaican lad, he had become the 'hero of the plebs'. The Cricket
Board, however, stood by its decision and Gilchrist wasn't included
in the team going to Australia.

On 30 January 1961, the MCC, who were touring in the Caribbean, played the West Indies at the Oval in Port of Spain and it became clear that they were going to win. The crowd watching the
match shouted their disagreement with and disapproval of some of
the decisions of the umpires. When it became obvious that the West
Indies were irredeemably on a losing wicket, the crowd started pelting the ground and the players with bottles in an attempt to stop the
match.

The incident was a national disgrace. It wasn't cricket. It was
an outpouring of nationalist resentment and plain bad behaviour.
James used the incident to write an open letter in *The Nation* to the
trustees of the Queen's Park Cricket Club, the owners of the club
under whose auspices the abortive test match had been played. He
turned the incident into a campaign for a commission of enquiry
into the disturbances and the deprivatization of the management of
cricket. He advocated an electoral college made up of the cricket
clubs throughout the island; this would elect a Board which would
replace the private club as the controllers of cricket.

James's argument was that, together with the movement towards
independence, cricket was the great public activity of the population of the West Indies and its management ought to be part of the
machinery of democracy.

It was perhaps the success of the campaign to win the captaincy
for Worrell that emboldened James to indulge in his intrigue against
Williams. The failure of the West Indian Federation in the months
before the West Indian islands were granted their independence left
James editing a paper which would remain the publication of a

Trinidadian Party instead of metamorphosing into the voice of the Caribbean. Jamaica and its politicians withdrew from the Federation and Eric Williams declared that 'one out of ten leaves nought'. Without the largest of the islands a federation of the smaller ones was doomed. The islands would go their own ways.

Undoubtedly the fall of the federal idea and consolidation of Eric Williams as sole Party leader and Prime Minister designate of Trinidad and Tobago when they gained their independence in 1962 contributed to the tension between him and James.

It was James's open agenda to be a citizen and leading philosophical light in a united federation of West Indian islands. He had accepted Eric Williams's invitation to edit the Party paper in the belief that the independence of the British Caribbean would lead to a West Indian federation whose power, success and political logic would then absorb Cuba, Martinique, Guadeloupe and the other small islands which were French, Spanish, Dutch or independent territories. Such a broad federation would have mineral wealth, adequate land and productive power, status in the world and, what's more, a potentially revolutionary peasant and labouring class who would keep at the least a watchful eye over the politicians leading the Caribbean to independence.

James had no faith in these politicians as the ultimate arbiters of the fate of the West Indies. In several essays he referred to them as the rootless bourgeoisie of the Caribbean, unfit to formulate any economic or indeed political strategy for the Caribbean. None of them originated in the labouring classes or the plantation owning classes of the islands: they came from the petty professional and essentially clerical class who wanted to make careers in colonial politics by gaining posts within the administration.

James felt that these politicians, none of whom understood the idea of federation, betrayed the Caribbean in pursuit of the small gain of jobs for themselves and their circle of supporters. If each island went its own way, each island could appoint a number of people to be ministers, ambassadors and the like. The motives for betrayal of the idea of federation were as petty as that. When the plans for a free federation fell apart, the idea of the Caribbean nation went with it. James wanted no part of serving a Trinidadian Party under the iron fist of his sometime pupil and friend Dr Williams.

In 1962, weeks before the independence celebrations, C.L.R. and Selma left Trinidad for London. Eric Williams became Trinidad's first Prime Minister.

In London James resumed his writing on cricket and his contact with the Facing Reality Group in America. He sent them the finished text of *Beyond a Boundary*.

From London he began writing about the politics of the newly independent West Indian islands. There was now no national Trinidadian realpolitik to restrain him. He wasn't in the Party about which he remained hopelessly optimistic. James wrote about Cuba, Haiti, Martinique and Guadeloupe, Puerto Rico and the Dominican Republic becoming part of the Federation of the West Indies. These countries, Cuba now under Castro, Haiti under the dictator Papa Doc Duvalier and Martinique and Guadeloupe annexed to France by de Gaulle, had not been part of the Federation envisaged through the decolonization of the British islands. He mooted the idea in an essay printed in *Freedomways* entitled 'Toward a Caribbean nation'.[1] It was an appeal to the Caribbean people above the heads of their politicians.

Then in 1965, without signalling his re-entry into the practical politics of the Caribbean, he returned to Trinidad. With George Weekes, the President of the Oilfield Workers Trade Union, and a Trinidadian Indian politician, Stephen Maharaj, he inaugurated the Workers and Farmers Party.

They launched a newspaper, *We, The People,* edited by James. The party declared itself opposed to Dr Eric Williams and the PNM, and for democratic rights, for the elimination of tensions between the Afro-Caribbean and the Indo-Caribbean population and the 'development of a nationally based economy'.

The mysterious return, in 1965, after what had been a humiliation for one who considered himself master of factional intrigue, was perhaps an attempt to cauterize the wound. It was also an attempt to prove that he had been correct all along. And more than that, it was an opportunity for revenge on a sometime pupil who had turned into a personal and political enemy.

Back in England, C.L.R. had begun to move in a circle of Caribbean writers and intellectuals based in London. The other islands were also gaining their independence and composing their anthems. It is possible that James thought that, even if he couldn't dethrone Eric Williams, he could give him a good run for his money.

His Workers and Farmers Party declared that it would put up candidates for every seat in the forthcoming national elections in Trinidad and Tobago. They campaigned throughout the island bitterly attacking the 'neo-colonial' policies of Eric Williams's ruling People's National Movement and promising the nationalization of the oilfields. The ballot was cast. C.L.R.'s party won barely 3 per cent of the national vote, and no seats. All of its candidates lost their deposits, including James who stood for his 'home' territory of Tunapuna and won 2.8% of the vote.

Eric Williams's Party, the PNM, won sixty-eight of the 100 seats in parliament. Badly beaten again by his old friend and new enemy, James returned to London.

In the early seventies, when there was a revolt in Trinidad and Tobago led by students and soldiers inspired by the rhetoric of American Black Power, the rebels contacted C.L.R. in London and he gave them advice about reading, training and tactics. The revolt got nowhere but it fired a warning shot across Eric Williams's bow. Dr Williams, apart from banning the works of C.L.R. James from the island, banned his *own* books, *Capitalism and Slavery*, an economic thesis proving that slavery in the West Indies contributed to the very formation of British industrial capital and *From Columbus to Castro*, a history of the Caribbean islands. Of his own books he said: 'They may give these half-educated Negroes the wrong ideas.'

10

Prospero's Island

I don't talk about my problems. Not to these people. I instruct. They obey. My daughter is the only one who comes close to understanding that these shoulders are burdened, weighed down. There is no pleasure in power and no escape. The Chinese say he who rides the tiger, etc.

But I can say with my hand on my heart that I didn't climb onto any tiger out of scheming ambition. Ever since I was a young man I felt the hand of Destiny on my shoulder and the world opened its doors. It was as though history was a secret attendant moving things for me. Education, the professorship, the return to Trinidad, the call to fight injustice and the elections, the decision of the British to go and leave us to it. The openings were irresistible. It was a trap. What shall I say? If I was literary like him, I would say 'O cursed spite, that ever I, Eric Williams, was born to put it right.'

He might have adapted the lines better. He had perfected that stuff. Shakespeare, Keats, that pornographer D. H. Lawrence, man! All got up for English and American women. How he loves them. How he has gone through life needing them. He wouldn't understand solitude. Not the solitude of office and authority.

It gets lonely on the hill, but perhaps the intelligent are lonely

everywhere. They teach themselves to talk, to charm, to be surrounded by flatterers. They dodge into argument and substitute
easy judgements for the painful conclusions that responsibility
brings. He has never had any responsibility. A son whom he abandoned, wives, political groupings made and destroyed by the same
charm and argument. I have built up my Party, my People's National
Movement, with no arguments. No one argues with me. Even he
wouldn't try. Not argue. He would challenge me to a public debate
where he could show off and gallery himself.

I must stop thinking about him. His chatter, his spurious scholas-
tics. His Bolshevik women.

From this house I can look down on Port of Spain and I can see
the moon above the sea, clean, serene. I tell you there are fellers
below in these shanties who look for me, who stalk my movements,
fellers with binoculars standing there below and trying to spot me
in my lair on the hill. I can hear them: 'De deaf ole coot on de hill.'

They see me walk around the garden, making notes of what to
tell these lazy good-for-nothing gardeners, and on a hot day they
may have seen me taking off my shirt. That led their excitable tem-
peraments and fiery minds to making up the stories which then
spread like a fire in a shanty. That I dance naked in the moonlight
with nothing but a stick and my hearing aid. Voodoo. The magic of
control. A sorcerer, a governor whose power is supernatural, un-
questionable. What would he say? He would say, 'Bill you have become Prospero?'

Dance with it? This damned earpiece slips out every few seconds
with the sweat in my ears. The heat of this island. I turn it off most
of the time. I don't want to hear their wails and screams, all sex and
beggary, all sex, violence and beggary.

They call it religion, they call it bacchanal, carnival, calypso, art,
even poetry, the idiom of the people. All sex, violence, criminality
and beggary. Their poverty is the real voodoo.

The damned racket from the tin shacks is maddening. These
fellers in my government, my 'cabinet', beasts and thieves to a man,

make speeches about moving the slums. They should move them. Away from my sight. Dynamite them. Tell the American missionaries to take them away.

I can't even get a replacement earpiece on the island. Have to send for it from my nephew in the States.

These slaves and the demons by which they are driven, emerging out of the circle of their lamp-lit houses, out of their black bottles. And he has come to make them feel worthwhile, human, part of civilization, with his cricket and his croaking about the people.

Son of a bitch. I know why he came back here. I thought I had sent him with his tail between his legs, back with his Jewess to poison the intellectual waters from which the gullible English drink, with their sympathy for the Negro everywhere.

He knows as well as I do that we need their fucking money, not their sympathy. But they don't want to part with money; they would rather extend 'solidarity'. Which of course plays into his hands. They play generous, he plays the wronged black feller. To the Negroes here he preaches about helping themselves, rising as a man. If two of them want to rise as a man, they should stop cutting each other with cutlasses over the same woman.

Oh yes, the Negroes will and must themselves and conquer this and that—vagueness, all vagueness. The world revolution, the instrument of the discontents of America. The Russians paid it lip service. But they didn't care about the world. The bastard is right, it can only succeed in the United States.

But we know his game. And it won't work here, not last time, not this time. This is my island, Mr James. My island in the sun where my people have toiled since time began and will go on doing so as long as I am in charge and can stand between them and your ideas of bringing them to my house to tear it down and then to dance around the fatted golden calf of your revolution.

A failure of a game, Mr James.

I know him well. He used to teach me when I was in school. A man without the guile to play a large game. Failed everywhere. And now he says he has come to . . . report a cricket tour. To report a cricket tour! He waves a letter. He has been commissioned by the *Observer* in London to cover the test match. Yes, the *Observer* in London. Must we be impressed. Our gates are flung open, our instincts supine.

He thinks I am an idiot. I can hear the island buzzing, humming. They are sharpening their knives, rehearsing their slogans and getting drunk. These Negroes don't know what independence means. To them it's revolt, the cutlass. And 'deafy' is clever, he achieved it with a few speeches. The whites have taken to their ships and gone.

Yes, they've gone. I have to piece together the wreck they left, but Mr World has returned to beguile the population, or those few who can spare the time from their debauchery to listen. He has dreams of bringing all the islands together, of declaring his socialist republic from Cuba to Curaçao. They will unite in good sense and belong to a nation at last.

A dream. I know these islands. I read about them, I write, I dream about the dank devils that wait for the congregations to emerge from the church door, the demons and spirits of those who died in violence. Everyone in the Caribbean died in violence.

That's our history. It's every man for himself. He knows that and still, and still . . .

Every night he goes down to speak to the oil men. He knows nothing about oil. Oil, oil, black gold, liquid gold, their eyes begin to shine like billiard balls. There's nothing in oil, man; there's too much of it in the world. We can't drink it. But there's no reasoning with these fellers. If the Yanks want our oil, it must be precious. No matter if the Yanks are just buying it to keep their own prices up. They could ban our oil, burn it. They are banning the sugar of Cuba. Who needs these islands? Only we do.

Please, gentlemen, please, some reason. Not all demagogy. When I invited him to come and help in 1958, he turns up and starts talking about nationalization. He tells me fifty:fifty and the oil companies jump at it. That's less than they give anywhere else in the world, for control mainly, for international control, but it sounds good to him. 'Fifty:fifty'. He can use it in a speech.

That's his problem, he will shoot his mouth off after filling it with anything that sounds good.

I'm waiting for it, man. The Negroes think, 'We have oil, let's keep it, sell it, get rich.' Why let the Yanks have it and make them rich? Simple economics, primitive reasonings. So now with Weekes and his trades union they will start all over again. Arguments are never won.

Good. I'm waiting. So I'll nationalize and the Americans, Italians, all of them, they'll pull out. They don't need our oil that badly. They'll leave us to drink it. I told Weekes and he understands but he's willing to play with the old fox, just to see whose tail is bushier.

If the old man is a fox, Weekes is a wolf. He knows about markets, distribution and who owns the petrol pumps. He won't let the old fox choke it all up. Honest men like Weekes work themselves up with a bucket and spade to be leaders of the Oilfield Workers Trade Union. Then they feel they've got to make trouble. But I know George, man. He won't throw all that away on some half-arse adventure. He knows that nationalization makes good speeches but bad policy.

Stop the oil, stop the oil? Uncle Sam, go to hell, we won't sell, we won't sell? All right, man, I hope your children like drinking oil. There won't be much other use for it. And then there may not be much more for them to drink, leave aside importation of claret for the old fox.

When I tell them that they tell me there's sugar. You look beyond the houses and the lanes where the bus winds up, there's sugar. Forty miles of it down to the south coast. Coolies with their stubbornness. Naked fakirs cutting their throats with their own cutlasses. I spend weeks selling the wretched crops, bargaining, fighting off the Cubans, Jamaicans.

Gratitude? In short supply, my friend. Like Lear's daughters, these Indians.

What puzzles me about the old fox is why he comes back. It's as though he doesn't know there's nothing for him here. He is deceived by the bullshit people surround him with. The great teacher, Confucius, pronounced 'confuse-us'. Why he don't stay in England and get his white women and his claret and music and everything. He can go to the theatre and play revolution. Those people pay to see the show.

How things change. I would have wished him with me if he had behaved himself. He doesn't know the meaning of loyalty.

He was my friend, my teacher, my guest in Washington. I kept him, I gave him money, I believed in half the things he said and I thought he was clever and wise enough to be, like me, ironic and sceptical of the other half.

And my mistake was I invited him to Trinidad. The threshold of a great adventure. Independence. We would have some years to build towards the raising of our flag and towards the day when we could run our own affairs. The British had no more stomach for it.

'Come and help build,' I said, Prime Ministerial stuff. He lands up here in Port of Spain. Old fox, with a long snout for smelling trouble. Trouble that he would make. 'Bill' was his name for me. He called himself Johnson and God knows what else. In Washington he calls me long distance from New York. He is ill and in trouble, he needs to see me. I could smell his desperation: could he come and stay for a few weeks, did I have any money to give him? I was glad to see him really. In Washington amongst the open Americans I missed the Trinidadian charm, the British manners of my old school. How we talked! Into each night, always about the world as it was and must be.

It's the way intelligent men have always talked to each other. There's no one to share it with now. These other fellers don't have half his wit. They bore me.

Then years later I call him home, willing to share with him. I expect him to understand. He betrays me. My stubbly hand, bitten as it fed.

My damn police are so corrupt they draw three salaries a week, from the Government, from the gangsters and smugglers and from the people who pay for protection against the gangsters. The army can't clean its own boots. The younger officers are no more than rebels from polite families wearing my uniform.

What is he after? Revolution? He would tell me himself, 'Bill'— no one called me Eric except my mother—'Trinidad is doomed. There is no revolution based on a little oil and a little sugar.'

I took him at his word. He didn't believe there could be a revolution here and still he wants to make trouble. It is me. It is me he is after. *L'état, c'est moi* in every sense now.

He tells the *Trinidad Guardian* that he has come back to report a cricket match. He can't play fast and loose here. We are both writers of history and know how quickly they can light fires in the Caribbean.

I am still writing that history while I am a prisoner of it.

'Does the Prime Minister know you are coming?' the customs feller asks him.

'I expect he has his spies and I hear that he knows everything, by magic. But I have a Trinidad passport, I can come and go,' he says.

But he is wrong. The British are no longer in charge. He can come when I allow and go when I say. L'état, c'est moi. I sent the gendarmes after him.

They've put him in his sister's house.

The long snout, man. He is relying on 'public opinion'. The public opines what I tell them to opine. He's had his arse kicked but one kick isn't a parable. He needs the next one.

'Williams Bans James.' That don't scare me, but I don't want to give him the satisfaction of even that. How he would love it. And he would spread the word that I tried to prevent the papers from printing the very headline he is reading. I can say to him, 'Yes, my friend, you are a citizen, you have a passport, you can come and go as you like for all to see.' I'm not huffing and puffing to fill his limp sail with wind.

He's been here six weeks now, wandering about the island, mind you, but confined after dark.

I told them to watch him, gently, if these wretched thugs of police understand the word. He hasn't tried any tricks yet. No meetings, a few people delivering messages, the usual stuff about newspapers, George Weekes going to see him and fellows from the Indian sugar belt sending him notes, but he doesn't reply. He has been a good boy.

Tomorrow I'll let him go. The papers will write about it. Then he can do interviews. Losers can talk. The *Observer* from London will call me, he'll make sure of that, and I will say 'James who? Our telephone directory is full of Jameses. A common name in these islands, sir. C.L.R.? Three initials? Very impressive. Is that Charlie, London, Radio? Good, good, good. A sports reporter? In Trinidad? Yes, cricket is of great interest to our people . . . you must excuse me. Duty calls. Being the Prime Minister I have no time for these stimulating discussions. Do speak to my secretary about Mr CFL Johns . . .'

I've got to sign some papers now—if only these clerks could spell . . .

He wrote me a last letter when he left the island. I have kept it.

> Bill,
> You have had a very easy time in politics. You don't know what political struggle is at all, in the internal party sense. That is what makes me now so nervous . . . I doubt if you are in any position for a variety of reasons to understand the reorganization of your party. If you do, you will do it under a sense of pressure. You are, I think at present, temperamentally disinclined to it . . .
>
> I don't want to be in that opposition where I will be one of the main advocates of a course that you will either refuse

to take or undertake, I am sure, with a sense of grievance and great irritation . . . I want to be out of this business.

That was the time when we were moving steadily towards being the only Party in charge of Trinidad and Tobago. It was I who had called him. 'Nello, man we need you, you have to come back, Things are happening and if people like you don't help we are doomed.'

'I don't understand your programme or policy,' he says.

His young wife is looking on, listening with her head forward like a spaniel, her ear cocked.

'All right,' I say. 'The policy is me!' That's what the people want. Remember Louis? It is me!

'Federation,' he says, 'I will come back if you commit us to the Federation. I will throw myself into it. It's the only way out for the small islands, unviable economies, marooned populations. Think what we can have, man. One sweep, call in Cuba and those French places eventually.'

'That's what I wanted you to come back as,' I said, quick as a flash, though it had never occurred to me before. 'We want to make you the editor of our newspaper. You will have a place in the governing party of the Federation.'

Was I bluffing? When I thought about it after putting the phone down, no, I wasn't. Maybe it would happen, but in politics there is no certainty. If there was a Federation, the international stature of it would demand an intelligent PM. There's nobody else. The Jamaicans would want everything, but we have the oil.

The thing to do with the fox is to make him think it was his idea in the first place. Never is a man so flattered as when he thinks others are following his plan.

He wasn't too bright. He was still a schoolmaster when I got my scholarship to Oxford and soon he followed me to England. He had no education abroad. He was a self-made feller, but he had made himself in the image of the world. If you met him in London, you couldn't tell from where James came, or what he didn't know. That was the trick of meeting other Negroes in London or Paris: to know what they were selling, what was the basis of their appeal in that white society.

Some were academic, some were accomplished, and others were handsome and suffering.

We met again in London, then in the United States when I went to Harvard to do my thesis, and every time I met him I was proud of him, my old schoolteacher and now my friend and mentor. He could out-talk any one in my circle, professors, lecturers, historians, he always knew more.

I wrote my thesis on capitalism and slavery and James pointed me in some directions. I got the figures, the pounds, shillings, pence, the economics I was writing about, but James gave me the twist, man. I don't take that away from him. To this day—I have arrested the son of a bitch and set him free—but to this day I will admit that he has the grand idea but he doesn't understand people. The evil in them.

His thesis worked. He said forget the religion, look at what actually happened. The British earned a lot of money from the slavery trade. They took it back to England and Scotland and began running industries. Slave capital was used to create the British working classes. It was a good thesis.

When he first called in New York, I had no idea he was in the States. We met in a flat he had been lent by some political sympathizer, two bare rooms on the Lower East Side. He said he was constantly on the move. He was wearing a vest and dirty trousers, stirring a saucepan full of beans. This was the man I had known as a gourmet in London, a man who taught me which claret to drink.

He came to me in Washington and lived in our house. Georgie was delighted with him, even though he talked our more conservative guests away. He would always preach, even in private conversation, but he would do it by asking me questions about myself and then proffering his advice. He was concerned about my intellectual dilemmas and always at hand with a solution.

He came for the last time when he was being thrown out of the

US. I could do nothing to help. I suggested that he write to Anthony Eden, the Foreign Secretary in the British Cabinet, begging his intervention. I said it to him as a joke.

He took it seriously and wrote the letter.

That was how foolish he had become. I should have read the signs. Eden's clerks replied saying that Eden could not agree that deportation to Britain was an undesirable fate.

When I quit Howard University and went back to Trinidad, I wrote to him. I had formed the People's National Movement on my own, man. I knew that Trinidadians were snobs, impressionable, rebellious, lacking bread and lacking circuses. I couldn't provide the bread at first but I resolved to provide the best circus in town.

I began to lecture in the central plaza of the capital, Woodford Square, in Port of Spain. The whole island began talking about it as the University of Woodford Square. The Calibans gathered to hear the music of Prospero. What folly had I sold myself? What exile had I chosen as I built this adulation, step by planned step; built the party, built my airy prison, brick by brick. Independent Trinidad, cut loose from the British ship of state, adrift with me as the captain. I should have wept. If I had real magic, better I should have drowned the island than chained myself to it. I threw in anything and everything I knew that would astound the Trinidadian public. I don't know how much of what I was saying they followed, but they were overjoyed. Their man, the doctor, was speaking: on the classics, on modern economics, on the history of Europe as it affected the history of the Caribbean. Each week the audience grew and with it grew the dedicated membership of the PNM. It was the first party in the world to float on hot air.

We were some way from independence but the Colonial Office, after the war and after the settlement of India, had been inclined to consider the issue and my talks with the Governor constantly ended with, 'Prepare yourself my boy, we don't intend to stay for ever.'

In London again I met with the others, with Norman Manley of Jamaica, Grantly Adams of Barbados and with Nello on whom each of these future Prime Ministers called. A federation they all said, but I sensed the hesitation, saw the teeth in the smile. What would the parliament be and what powers would the constitution give to the islands?

It was a game. We knew that we would go our ways but the Colonial Office and James fell for the tale and waited for the details.

That was when the old fox's lectures began. He said we were an expectant people with resources. That should have been an alarm bell, but I trusted the feller. That word 'expectant'. Yes of course. I knew the Bolshevik.

When I called him in 1958 in his London flat, where the bill for the phone had not been paid and where as a consequence he couldn't be reached till other friends walked in and saved the situation, he said he would come straight away. He had been waiting for the call. He should have paid his phone bill.

The PNM paid the passage. He came with his young wife and set himself up in his sister's house. When he arrived, I tell you, he was amazed at what he saw the PNM doing. I was speaking at a rally in the south the next day, talking about anti-colonialism and the terms on which we would have it. There were all sorts there, the blacks and the light-skinned fellers, standing, like a cattle auction in a corral. The old Bolshevik was astounded.

'With a movement like this, man, you can do anything.'

That night it came to me. We wanted him as an ally not as mischief. All his life he had been the rat gnawing at the moorings, chewing away, saying 'no', making other people strike, resist, destroy—now was the time to build! Could he cross over? I called him and flattered him, always a good thing. I called him 'maestro' and 'guru' and he loved it.

I offered him the job of Secretary of the West Indian Federal Labour Party and he said yes, he would like that. I made up the organization on the spot and made a few phone calls to the others in Jamaica and British Guiana. Before he began to act for the Federation and as soon as he got a taste of the fact that there was a mass movement here, he came to me and said he was anti-leadership, he was a Marxist, but he would curb his tendencies and we could see how it went.

There was this feller Carlton Comma in charge of the library and he was in trouble with the Party. My deputies were gunning for him, politically and personally. So what he does is invite James to give a series of lectures.

The first lecture is packed out. People standing outside with the loudspeakers. He talks about the role of the proletariat. He talks about the end of colonialism and the weakness of the imperial countries.

By the time he gets to the sixth lecture, there aren't many people listening. He comes back to me. He wants to join the PNM and he will do what he can do best. I invite him to talk to me about the policies of the Party.

'Just like old times, man,' he says.

I knew he would be useful. And he'd behaved himself like a tame bear. We could set him to fight the old communists and diehards who would bark and snap at the Party from the left. I proposed that he edit and run the Party newspaper, and he said he'd take that but he wanted to rename it and call it *The Nation*. Always the big canvas.

Those were heady days. The rest of the Party told me not to trust him. He was a snake lying in the basket, but he would sneak out and sting later. He would try to take control, he was paid by Russia and so on. He knew more than all of them put together and more than their grandfathers.

We had to have a programme and policy and I called him to my villa at the beach. He wrote the whole thing in two days. I read it and revised it three times. He wrote it as I wanted it in the end. One idea he wanted to keep: 'We must build our party organization from the bottom up.' Whose bottom?

I let him keep it, it sounded good. It would affect nothing. I knew I was the Party. I had built this Party. Nothing stirred in it without my sanction. No one was allowed to speak on a platform saving myself, until they became candidates for parliament, hand-picked by me. He could write what he liked. That would be the Party policy. If I said so.

You know what surprised me? He seemed to believe what he had written. He wasn't crazy. But he was no politician. A man of words. Words that could reach the people, he thought, move the world.

That was the challenge. I would give him the gift of words, I would retain the privileges of office. We would see who won. Yes, oh yes, I knew that in his heart he wanted to win, to see me defeated. By what or whom, he didn't know. But it would be Williams versus words. So I gave him the words.

'Nello, Chief, would you like to edit the Party's paper? You have a free hand.'

He didn't know it was a challenge, or if he did, he took it with oaths of loyalty.

He kept his promises. The paper came out more or less regularly and with writing on history, economics, the doings of the Party, membership columns, letters columns, and the campaigns. This wife of his was the force behind the paper. She kept it punctual. Kept a hold of the money.

This was how it went. The old man edits and sends out Walter Anamanthodo to spy on everyone and find out who is saying what. And all the time Selma is in charge of the arrangements. The workers on the paper itself don't like that. They are supposed to be in charge, not the whites. Some of them start giving trouble.

'Who is she to come here and boss us about?' But no one pays them any attention because it's a good paper.

Then he starts this business about a black captain for the West Indian cricket team. I say good. We nominate Frank Worrell and we win it. Nello writes and pushes. The paper becomes popular. 'The black Caribbean is capable of captaincy in all spheres. Let's begin with cricket.'

On the tip of the island in the north is a place called Chaguaramus, the old Carib name. It was his idea to make an issue of it, a stunt before the elections. You see there was an American naval base there, loaned by the Colonial Office to the Yanks after the war. It was a great symbolic idea. I marched on the base with 50,000 people behind me.

'Yankee go home. Massa day done.'

They asked me in for talks. Fifty thousand dollars? They didn't want to shoot on the people. They would give up half the land and pay rent for the rest. These Negroes understand rent. 'Rent,' they went around saying. 'De Doc get them to pay rent.'

'What do you think, Nello?'

'Say no. All or nothing,' he said. 'The people want them to go and you'll win a huge following.'

The idiot didn't realize I couldn't say no. I didn't need a larger following at that point. The election was secure. The PNM had more than 60 per cent of the vote. He confused the prose with the passion.

I did the deal.

He didn't like it but he swallowed it. No trouble. Even his paper said OK for now.

At this time he was being invited all over the Caribbean to speak and he spoke about Federation. That's when he got a bit cocky, when crowds turned up in Barbados and Grenada to listen. He talked about Jamaica, Guyana and Trinidad committing themselves to the Federation of islands immediately.

Jamaica. Norman, old Busty, their warhorse Prime Minister, didn't like the idea. Jamaica was too big to be just one more partner in a federation. The Jamaicans always swaggered. I wasn't for the Federation idea but I went along with it. I could have been Prime Minister of a whole Caribbean Federation. It was a dream and harmless talk, but the Party became suspicious of brother James.

The man came back thinking he could launch a challenge with this Federation nonsense. A challenge against me! He had gone mad. He started spreading subversion.

As they would say, 'De bwoy get licks on Chaguaramus. So him come in de house and bawl.'

I didn't realize that he was still smarting from the fact that I had accepted rent instead of kicking the Yankees out. He wanted an international gesture, the Yankees to pack their bags and flags and depart the island.

Mr James started a secret campaign for 'party democracy'. In the land of the deaf Premier there are no secrets. He was doing what he promised he wouldn't do. He was back to his Marxist tricks man, demanding greater participation in the paper and in the Party, in heaven and in hell. The boys didn't like it. They said, 'End of the line for James.'

In the October meeting of the Party he was expelled for mismanagement of the Party paper, its funds, its schedules, its workers, its sales. They wanted to say he was a traitor and all this, but I said 'leave it at mismanagement, boys'. They said what mismanagement? I said there was bound to be some, go and find it. The people would believe that. If we kick him out for treachery, it will give these idle people some drama. They will get excited. Mismanagement is a good little crime.

Three weeks before the Party kicked him out, he had seen the writing on the wall. He called me and said he couldn't carry on and he wrote a letter resigning from *The Nation*.

He knew that I knew what he had been carrying on with. Anamanthodo warned him that I had discovered his little back-biting intrigues. How could he mess with the People's National Movement? Who the hell is James? I called him in. I told him I knew all about his clique in San Fernando and all his prattle about democracy. The man was absurd. He had even told them that he would challenge me for the leadership of the Party.

Those boys in the south led him on. 'Oh Mr James, we read your books. Fine books, man.'

There was a schoolteacher called Nicholas Simonet in the Party in the south. He had a few dissatisfied fellers round him, grumbling about how Port of Spain people get the big jobs and bribes. I summoned Simonet. I had him brought up here.

'So what is it you plan to do, Nicky boy?'

'Oh nothing, Dr Williams, nothing. What could we do? I would not want to do anything.'

'Well, I'm glad to hear it man. I heard you have some dissatisfactions. That you've been shooting your mouth man, all about how the south own the cow and the north milking it. That's an old beef, young feller,' I said.

I wanted to terrorize the little *maqquero*.

'What is it you boys don't have down there? You want to discuss all that in the economic committee.'

'Of course, sir, that's right.' He was scared like hell.

'That's right is it? Then what are you doing gallerying with the old man.'

'Old man, which old man?'

'Which old man? Nicky, I tell you, you Negroes will never learn. You held six meetings, you talked about a challenge. One of your own fellers come and tell me. He is not your feller, he is my feller. Now you want to resign from the Party?'

'No, sir. I want to stay.'

'You want to stay and challenge for the leadership. You want to be Premier, eh Nicky? You must tell me, where you are going to challenge and with whom? I have to be on my guard, man, have some mercy on a deaf man,' I said.

'All loose talk, sir, loose talk.'

'Well you tell the others to tighten up that talk. I will see to Mr James, Mr Karl Marx, and mamma Lenin himself. Now go and don't let me hear anything more from you, Nicky, boy. You are a schoolteacher aren't you? You must have heard the proverb, little boys should be seen and not heard. A good proverb.'

'Yes sir,' he says.

When it came to the Party conference, the old man had no votes. Not one. Nicky and his San Fernando boys who had talked to him by candlelight had vanished with the dawn. He was alone.

I took him aside. I said 'Nello, I have known you a long time. Don't be foolish. This is my Party, I built it. It is a one man party. You know some theory. I know how to run a party. Now fuck off.'

I was never normally crude, but he understood.

The conference expelled him as I had directed, 'in absentia for mismanagement'.

He stayed in Trinidad for a while. If he gave a lecture somewhere, I sent my boys and got reports. He had no following. The army could sleep peacefully in its barracks that night. They wouldn't be needed to suppress the revolution.

I heard later that, before the independence celebrations, James and his wife slipped away, like thieves in the night. This wasn't their country.

All that was two years ago and now for the 1960 cricket tour he sneaks back. He is entitled. Britain plays the West Indies right here. I shall go to the cricket match myself and if I see him, I'll call him to lunch. I'll ask him how he gets his money, who pays him nowadays. Maybe he's hungry.

11

Who Is Lebrun?

Before he embarked on this final electoral adventure, James had settled in London with Selma. They set up house in Willesden in the north-west of the city and this house became a centre for West Indians in exile, artists and writers who had come away in the sixties, as James had in the thirties, hoping to make their name and get their books published or their paintings exhibited in the metropolis. Among these exiles was the young V. S. Naipaul, who had come to Oxford as an island scholar and stayed on to write his brilliant, original, acclaimed novels.

James Baldwin once wrote in an essay that when two blacks meet each other at the cocktail party that is the European literary scene they eye each other and circle each other. Each can be seen thinking, 'How did he get here? What's his hustle?' And they circle each other because each is terrified that the other will 'knock his hustle', will make plain to the party that the other is there on false pretences.

This may well have been true of James and Naipaul, who never seem to have become personally much more than wary acquaintances. The literary connections between them, however, are significant and interesting.

Both James and Naipaul were born and brought up in British

colonial Trinidad, although a generation removed from each other.
Both came away to England. Each conceived a literary ambition
while still on the island. Literary ambition led to concerns and
achievements that placed both of them on a wider stage than that of
their island origins. Neither returned home for good.

Both writers celebrated their escape from the Caribbean. V. S.
Naipaul's very early and valedictory book, *A Middle Passage,* made
it clear that the islands could not contain his ambitions. There was
nothing of him there.

James's view of his island homelands was similar. He characterized the islands as 'pieces of dirt in the Caribbean', and mitigated
his contempt for them by describing their populations as 'twentieth-century people trapped in a seventeenth-century economy'.
Sometimes in private talks he'd go further: 'These Barbadian boys.
I've seen them. All they can do is put perfume in their hair and sell
themselves on the beach to rich old white American women. That is
degradation indeed, man!'

It was James's constant and probably his only source of pride in
Trinidad and the Caribbean that its marginal colonial culture had
produced writers of international stature like Vidya Naipaul. He
would mention George Lamming, Wilson Harris and Derek Wal-
cott, but, with the exception of *An Area of Darkness,* he would acknowledge that his reputation and work stood above the rest.

It is not surprising that they reviewed each other's books. James
reviewed Naipaul's *The Mystic Masseur* in the *New Statesman* and
Naipaul was captivated by the insightful attention that James gave
the book. He considered that the review was penetrative because it
noticed that this comic novel was an entirely new way of looking at
the Caribbean and that the writer's gift and perspective deserved
congratulation. They told a truth that had never been told.

In turn, Naipaul reviewed James's *Beyond a Boundary.* Later,
however, James became acutely critical of Naipaul's first book about
India, *An Area of Darkness.* For James it was a disappointed and
bitter book, although sharply observed. In public, C.L.R. dismissed
it with the words: 'What is he talking about? How can the country

of Gandhi and Nehru be an Area of Darkness? Naipaul is saying what the whites want to say but dare not. They have put him up to it.'

A Way in the World, Naipaul's partly-autobiographical novel published in 1994, sheds more light on the relationship. Naipaul says he met James in 1962 and he writes of a meeting in C.L.R.'s house, real or partly imaginary:

> It was all immensely intelligent and gripping. He talked about music and the influence on composers of the instruments of their time. He talked about military matters. I had met no one like that from our region, no one who had given so much time to reading and thought, no one who had organized so much information in this appetizing way . . . it was rhetoric, of course. And of course it was loaded in his favour. He couldn't be interrupted, like royalty, he raised all the topics; and he would have been a master of all the topics he raised.

Most significant, however, is the character of Lebrun in *A Way of the World,* which Naipaul has admitted in conversations with me was at least partly inspired by James. The details of Lebrun's life, his birth in Central America and his relationship with Africa are not the same as James's, but there is no mistaking the character Naipaul describes, nor the early salon at 'Lebrun's' home. He was there.

Our first introduction to Lebrun in *A Way in the World* is when the young Naipaul remembers an unread book by Lebrun, in his senior school library cupboard; it is a historical book about General Miranda.

If Naipaul modelled the unread Lebrun book on *The Black Jacobins,* he introduces a double-edged irony when, at the end of *A Way in the World,* he himself tells the story of Miranda, devoting a whole section of the book to the very story that fellow pupils left on the bottom shelf, unread. Is Naipaul taking the book from the school library shelf and dusting it off? Or is he inviting us to compare his chapter on Miranda the adventurer with *The Black Jacobins* and, if so, why? Perhaps in order to point out that the 'revolutionaries' of the region were sad and tragic frauds and not the heroes that legends, including C.L.R. James's 'history', has made them?

There are too many similarities between the Lebrun and James's stories not to see the book as, in part, Naipaul's assessment of his fellow Trinidadian. Lebrun, for instance, first gets to know Naipaul when he writes a review of his work—his first and second comic novels in a Russian journal. Naipaul, startled with the flattering and penetrating piece of analysis, records his reaction:

> It was as though, from moving at ground level, where so much was obscured, I had been taken up some way, not only to be shown the pretty pattern of fields and roads and small settlements, but also, as an aspect of that high view, had been granted a vision of history speeded up, had seen as I might have seen the opening and dying of a flower, the destruction and shifting about of peoples, had seen all the strands that had gone into the creation of the agricultural colony, and had understood what simple purposes—after such activity—that colony served.

Despite this fresh gift of insight, Naipaul's Lebrun doesn't go on to do more of the same for other people, for other writing, for other phenomena. Instead he goes on to leech off white people, to flit from one ex-colony to the other, flattering ruthless and stupid dictators with big words, goading them on to acts of revolutionary destructiveness and then moving on, never living with the consequences and catastrophes his words and ideas have catalyzed.

This becomes clearer when, later, Lebrun meets Naipaul in London, at a Maida Vale salon where people have gathered to hear the revolutionary speak and when, later still, Naipaul is invited to dinner by some friends of Lebrun's, in New York. There he finds the talk influenced by Lebrun's views and 'political resolution'. It becomes clear to Naipaul that this Lebrun pays his way through the promise of a Caribbean revolution to come. He makes himself interesting to the international hosts who flatter and finance him, by promising, as every con man does, that astounding events will flow from his analysis. The years pass, however, and the revolution that Lebrun promises never comes. The hosts tire of the parasite. Naipaul consigns his character to living in old age off the bounty of women admirers, finding himself 'lodging in other people's houses or apartments in the Caribbean, and Central America, in England and Europe, and always moving on'.

The description of how the West Indian islands disclaim Lebrun is also closely reminiscent of James's own experience after the Caribbean islands gained their independence. The intellectuals and trades union leaders in the islands who formed parties and came to power knew of James's adventures with Williams and they wanted nothing of C.L.R. He was trouble. In the narrative, Lebrun went to one of the islands where he attempted to dominate the Prime Minister and the ruling party. When the plot was discovered he was thrown out, and the Prime Minister said of Lebrun 'the man want to take you over'.

Naipaul sees the irony. He says, 'Once the person who was now Chief Minister would have been flattered by Lebrun's attentions. He would have loved the big technical-sounding words Lebrun would have used to describe the simple movement he had got going.'

Cruel though it may sound, Naipaul's assessment of Lebrun as 'an impresario of revolution', had some basis in James's relationship with the newly independent Caribbean leaders. Like Lebrun, he 'had no base of his own, no popular following. He always had to attach himself to other leaders, simpler people more directly in touch with the simple people who had given them power, and with a simpler idea of that power.'

Naipaul's writing is rooted in the Caribbean. His novels, his historical account of the colonial settlement of Trinidad are all set there. In *Guerrillas* and *The Killings in Trinidad*, Naipaul explored and exposed another kind of Caribbean fraudulence in fiction and in non-fiction. Each concerns one Michael de Freitas, another Trinidadian who had come to Britain. As the self-styled Michael X, de Freitas became a Black Power leader. Through a lazy and violent rhetoric he gained a following amongst rich whites who assuaged their own feelings of guilt towards black people by paying him money. He finally went back to Trinidad with an upper middle-class white woman, whom he murdered and buried in the 'commune' which he ran with two deluded young men from the island and an American adventurer calling himself Jamal Ali.

By the time he wrote *A Way in the World* in 1994, after C.L.R. James was dead, Naipaul had transferred some of the rage he felt at the fraud, waste and cruelty of the Caribbean to the personality of Lebrun. It was as though he suspected that something of the secret of the contemporary Caribbean could be confronted and explained by getting to the core of a character like C.L.R. James. Or not even 'like' C.L.R. James, but to the man himself. Naipaul's Lebrun is C.L.R. James with something of the adventurer and black power leader Stokely Carmichael thrown in.

It is, of course, easy to confound C.L.R. with the black demagogues that rose with him to fame on the shoulders of the Black Power movement. Some of these, such as Stokely Carmichael, whose behaviour and pronouncements certainly influenced Naipaul's portrait of Lebrun, were ambivalent about the brutality of Africa personalized in figures like Idi Amin and in the dictatorships of Houphet-Boigny and other savage and primitive despots.

James's view of such despots paralleled Naipaul's, but James had put himself in the ambiguous position of accepting the discipleship of dubious followers and practitioners of a brutal politics.

One of the 'revolutions' of the Caribbean that called itself 'Jamesian', and is a clear example of the inspiration to mischief which Naipaul had in mind when describing Lebrun's revolutionary activities, took place in Grenada in 1979. This insurrection ended in 1983 in a bloody and dramatic episode.

In 1995, I went with a crew to Grenada to research a film on the Grenadan insurrection.

Our film's story began with the coup mounted by the New Jewel Movement against the Government of Eric Gairy, in 1979. In 1983, the comrades who pulled the coup split into factions and murdered each other. Claiming that they had been called in by neighbouring countries to restore democracy, the Americans landed marines. In 1995 we found that Eric Gairy, the deposed dictator of 1979, was standing for re-election at the head of the Party he had headed when he was Prime Minister—the Grenada United Labour Party, or GULP—which was also my reaction to the fact.

After days of negotiation we were granted an interview with Gairy. We went to a house in Grand Anse which had been converted into a 'hotel' with three holiday chalets built next to its drive and a wicker hut in the garden which served as a tropical bar. We settled round a table in a room opening onto the lawn. Finally Sir Eric appeared: an old man, dressed completely in white—shirt, trousers, shoes, socks. He stepped out of a car accompanied by a tough-looking young man who was obviously his bodyguard.

Sir Eric was blind. He was escorted to our table, walking, or rather shuffling along, and stretched out his hand into the void for each of us to shake in turn while introducing ourselves. We said we wanted his side of the Grenada story.

'If I had known that, I wouldn't have led you a dance,' he said. 'This is what I *want* to talk about.'

We put the questions to him. Was he running a tyranny before the coup? What was this 'Mongoose Gang' in his employ? Didn't the new government that replaced him by force meet with instant public approval?

Gairy disdained to answer a single question directly. He said there was no 'Mongoose Gang'. It was a term his enemies used, but he told us the etymology of it. During his regime, the World Health Organization (WHO) had come to Grenada to instruct the people on how to eliminate pests. The environmental workers employed to trap mongooses came to be known as the 'Mongoose Gang'.

Accurate, perhaps, but we knew Gairy was using the explanation to avoid answering our original question—hadn't the Mongoose

Gang behaved like his personal paramilitary force, threatening, maiming and killing—Tonton Macoute!

He was a very good actor, and he put on this speechifying tone, as though talking to a crowd of thousands: 'Forty cents an hour? No! Never!' It was powerful, hamming. We were vaguely embarrassed, but gave him some fake compliment. He went on: 'I am the chosen one. Oh yes. Eric Gairy has nineteen knighthoods. Nineteen, you know. And the miracles. His life is a miracle! God put me here to do the job and I will do it. When I do the job, God will restore my sight.'

It was, doubtless, someone like Gairy, if not Gairy himself, whom Naipaul visited and who told him that 'Lebrun' was not welcome on his island, who boasted that he would see him off because 'The man want to take you over.'

Lebrun is not, however, totally modelled on James. There are very particular and significant ways in which the two diverge.

Lebrun's dedicated Sovietism is a feature which cannot be attributed to James. It is Naipaul's simple way of characterizing his character as a communist; the refinement of being a Trotskyist and anti-Soviet would have added confusion to contempt. Likewise, the comparison of Lebrun and the influence of Black Power does not hold much water. Like Lebrun, James did gain some attention through the intervention of Black Power, but he rode that storm as a witch does, on a frail broomstick, ahead of all the darkling clouds, lightning and gunfire flashing all around him.

The real James knew he was not 'Black Power'. He was a writer who predicted the implosion of the Soviet empire. He was the writer who espoused and championed the Western intellectual tradition as the direction and salvation of modernity and the world, including Africa. He was the man of the colonies whose intellect educated itself to defeat colonialism and grew to inspire merciless criticism of the regimes that succeeded colonial rule. Black Power wasn't a movement equipped to grasp any of these propositions from C.L.R.'s life and writing.

The era of Black Power came and went. C.L.R. had, through the dynamic of this era perhaps, a professorship at Howard University in Washington and a pension from it. He was invited by many such faculties of universities the world over, but he was never shamelessly opportunistic and stuck to his qualified approvals and to his idea that all history was not black and white.

The importance of Lebrun is that Naipaul wanted to place a particular sort of Caribbean personality in its historical context, to put to rest a ghost. To have written is to have done with. And as one reads there is the sneaking realization that the writer, Naipaul, is wary of this character, the contemplation of whose life and acts fills him with something akin to loathing. Perhaps the writing is an effort to purge loathing with understanding, to look the ghost straight in the face and even see if he can muster any sympathy for it.

He is someone Naipaul has to confront in his factual-fictional form. He is larger than life in his revolutionary ambition and in his grasp of Western culture. He is a unique figure from Naipaul's world, one who embodies finally the tragedy of rootlessness, a condition imposed by history, which Naipaul acutely feels.

James's interaction with Wilson Harris, the Guyanese writer, is altogether simpler, but more puzzling to me. James cultivated a friendship with him, read his work and asked if he could 'contribute to its critical appreciation'. When he went back to Trinidad in 1965 for his electoral adventure and debacle, he lectured on this writer's work at the University of The West Indies.

This essay in criticism began with a difficult exposition of the philosophy of Heidegger and Jaspers. It then progressed to claim that Wilson Harris is the novelistic embodiment of their philosophy and that he has important things to say about the West Indian novel. James quoted these passages of importance and left the audience, as well as this reader, totally baffled.

Somewhere in the vision of C.L.R. James is a blind spot. Every cook may be able to govern, but every cook is not bound to understand the obscurities of Wilson Harris. C.L.R.'s speeches were in the main crystal clear, sometimes simplistic. Yet something made him champion the work of Wilson Harris who is at best a mystic with faltering English and at worst a fraud.

Here's Wilson Harris talking to an audience of West Indian students in London in the mid-sixties. James was in the audience and reported the occasion.

> And this vision of consciousness is the peculiar reality of language because the concept of language is one which continuously transforms inner and outer formal categories of experience, earlier and representative modes of speech itself, the still life resident in painting and sculpture as such, even music which one ceases to 'hear'—the peculiar reality of language provides a medium to see in consciousness the 'free' motion and to 'hear' with consciousness the 'silent' flood of sound by a continuous inward revisionary and momentous logic of potent explosive images evoked in the mind. Such a capacity for language is a real and necessary one in a world where the inarticulate person is continuously frozen or legislated for in mass and a genuine experience of his distress, the instinct of distress, sinks into a void. The nightmare proportions of this already becoming apparent throughout the world.[1]

James reported on this passage with a gush of enthusiasm:

> Whom Harris has been reading I don't know. I sent him at once a copy of my Heidegger and he rapidly replied that he

agreed with Heidegger entirely. The point that shook me was that Harris, grappling with a West Indian problem, had arrived at conclusions which dealt with the problem of language as a whole in the world at large.

Harris's meaning is unclear. It is tempting to call the whole thing deliberately obscure and this temptation is encouraged by a reading of the rest of Wilson Harris's work. I don't know what the sentences mean and can't make sense of the whole. But in trying to pull meanings from Harris's work, James extracted a political point.

The novels of Harris, claimed James, point to a uniquely West Indian phenomenon. The islands were founded in violence and lack the lingering morality of the Middle Ages that still haunts Europe. Without those ghosts, more things are possible in the Americas, in the Indies, than are dreamt of in European philosophy. These territories doubted the presence of the European God before Nietzsche declared him dead.

James saw the twentieth century, starting with the slaughter of the First World War, then the Stalinist gulags and the Holocaust, as the most violent in history. The twentieth century constantly poses a choice. History is always in dispute. One man's justice is another man's barbarism. It may even be that, in pointing down the road to socialism, the 'socialist' historian may overlook a barbarism or two. James's uncritical acceptance of Lenin as the prophet is a case in point. But historians of a different inclination may insist on dragging horrors out of their closet and laying them at Lenin's door.

James's written work, over six decades, could form the backbone of several courses of lectures, more radical, more refreshing, more endowed with historical and critical method and insights, than some of the spurious scholarship that's peddled as black history in the universities of the world. If he had compromised he would have deserved the name 'Lebrun'.

12

A Straight Bat

In October 1960 James sent the manuscript of *Beyond a Boundary* from Trinidad to John Arlott, the famous cricket commentator and editor of sports books, with a view to having it published. It was returned to him even though Arlott wrote an extremely complimentary letter declining the chance to publish. He said that the market for such a book was uncertain and only the autobiographies of famous players and the cricket writing of Neville Cardus stood a commercial chance of success. James was, of course, disappointed. To him, the book was more than a collection of thoughts on cricket.

Beyond a Boundary is unique. It is not simply autobiography through sport, but more a personal work of history. The task James set himself was to tell the story of cricket and in so doing to comment on the role of games of mass popularity in social evolution.

James compared cricket, its organization and its popularity, to the Olympic Games of ancient Greece. He was surprised when he set out in this quest to note that the English, into whose national life the game had become integrated, had not written serious books about it. Of course, there were hundreds of books about particular games and particular cricketers, biographies of players, studies of scores, statistics and so on. But there was no book tracing the connection of sport to social movements.

But for James interest in organized sport went hand in hand with the mass instinct for democracy and in *Beyond a Boundary* he gives us a quick historical sketch of some eras in history. He begins with the Greek city states, moving on to the rise of cricket at the time of the Reform Bill in England, and the relationship of the nationalist movement and the growth of cricket in the British colonies of India and the West Indies.

Trotsky believed that organized sport was the opium of the people, a distraction for the working class. With all that he had seen and learned in the USA, C.L.R. begged to differ: 'With my past I simply could not accept that. I was British. The organizational drive for sport had come from Britain. It was from Britain that cricket, and soccer more than cricket, has spread as nothing international had ever spread for centuries before.'[1]

After his time as an American Bolshevik, James was brave to admit that he had not revised his view of his ethical origins. The world had changed and was about to change further. There was to be a major challenge to the old order, to the systems of value that cherish the family at home.

Beyond a Boundary is essentially about ethics and art, and while James acknowledges that his ethics derive from the inherent ideas of fair play embodied in the game of cricket, and that his world view is Western, he questions the concept of art. What is art, he baldly asks. He gives us the answer he favours, which would include in the same breath as Michelangelo's judgement and brush stroke, the bowling action and assessment of the required batting stroke by a cricketer.

The central historical thesis of the book is that the British aristocracy gave way to the British bourgeoisie who turned the game of cricket into the ethical metaphor of their tribe. They were the colonizers, the products of public schools and the code they exported was received and transformed by those they colonized.

James had read *Death in the Afternoon,* Hemingway's classic on bullfighting, even though he had made it plain throughout his life that he hated blood sports, despised boxing and would not visit a zoo. He did admire Muhammad Ali, though, and when, in his final years he asked for a satellite dish so that he could receive Sky TV, I always suspected that it was so that he could secretly watch the heavyweight fights.

In *Death in the Afternoon,* Hemingway brought the great gladiatorial sport into his discourse about life and death. His descriptions and fancies combined the popularity of bullfighting in Spain with an existential ethic that subsumed the questions of right and wrong in this battle, to the aesthetics of a skilled dance of death.

James confessed that he admired Hemingway's writing and the thesis of the book even though he found bullfighting barbaric. 'Hemingway is right to say that grace and form are given to this act of cruelty,' he said. 'Cricket does the same thing for the West Indies, you know. It adds style and grace and elements of culture to a society which has little else of the kind.'

Beyond a Boundary finally found a publisher in Hutchinson in mid-1961. James had sent a manuscript to George Lamming, a Guyanese novelist living in London, and he took it to Robert Lusty, the Chairman of Hutchinson. It was reviewed and received well, in Britain and in the Caribbean. James was a writer again and he basked in it. V. S. Naipaul wrote a good review in *Encounter* and James wrote back thanking him for it. Its acceptance and publication by Hutchinson were for James the reassertion of his cultural self. He had given himself in autobiography the two identities with which he had begun—cricketer and writer. He had not at this stage experienced the rejection of the Trinidadian electorate and was confident of his powers.

The same George Lamming used James and Selma as prototypes in his own novel, *Natives of My Person.* The character modelled on

James is called Surgeon. His wife is the faux naive narrator, the 'Selma' character speaking:

> It was such a noble sight. Men of learning collaborating on a plan. And my husband at the centre of their attention. He was always like that. It was his natural place. At the centre of their attention. I would serve them food and drink. But I could not partake of their analysis. Their talk was always above my understanding, and I was the substance of their concern. I and all who might be victims of any sickness in the Kingdom. To hear them predict the future that could come if circumstances allowed their plans to operate, it was like waiting for heaven.[2]

Lamming has slyly inserted his own scepticism about the Jamesian agenda. And he has got Selma wrong.

Selma was and is by no means someone who would acknowledge that the talk of any group passed over her head. Neither would it. She was a helper, a sounding board, a typist, a participator and, in the end, a rival.

In 1968, when Paris exploded in student revolt, James visited the city. His analysis of the uprising was enthusiastic but tempered. While welcoming its energy and seeing it as a vindication of his approach to revolutionary change, he now saw that it was difficult or virtually impossible to prescribe its direction. The revolutionary had to wait and watch what the mass of people wanted.

In C.L.R.'s view by that time, whatever large groups of people do—with the exception, of course, of joining parties that murder Jews or Christians or put women behind veils—contains the potential for larger revolts. There was one caveat introduced from his reading of Lenin. A situation becomes revolutionary when the people taking part attempt to transcend the highest point of activity reached by their predecessors in the history of their workplace or country. For the people of the Soviet Union and its satellites, the challenge would be to transcend the Hungarian uprising of 1956 which generated spontaneous and heroic attempts by the citizens of Budapest and then by the whole country to shake off the Russian yoke. The revolution was finally crushed by the presence of invading Russian tanks, but it left its mark on history and James predicted, most accurately as it happened, that some section of Hungarian, Polish, Rumanian or Bulgarian society would go further than that and that this would lead to the demise of the Soviet power in that country. The flaw in the argument is that it seems to be saying where you land is your destination, and this makes it impossible to chart the effect that political organization has on change.

From his base in London, James returned in the seventies to lecture in Washington at Howard University. He also lectured at campuses in New York and became something of a celebrity in limited academic circles.

In 1973 I visited him in his flat in Washington to do an interview for the British Black Panther Movement magazine. Selma had remained in England and James was being looked after by a young man who took a long time to undo all the locks, the security precautions, that had been installed on the door.

'What's the danger?' I asked C.L.R. at the beginning of our interview.

'You don't know what they will do,' C.L.R. replied, with genuine urgency. 'They come to rob you and they'll break the door down. I don't go out at all, man, and I advise you to leave before dark.'

I didn't know whether this was a ruse to get shot of me or genuine advice.

We talked for a few hours. He sat in his bed surrounded by books and papers and he enquired about the progress of the movement in Britain.

He was very interested in detail. I had determined to ask him about his political prognostications, but he turned the conversation skilfully to me. He asked me about myself, where I was educated and what I was reading. Then he asked about the Movement.

I had resolved not to divulge a great deal of the internal differences that had arisen in the group. I summed it up for him. Some of the group wanted to 'get active', by which they meant some sort of terrorist activity in imitation of the Irish Republican Army. Others wanted to transform the whole Movement into a self-help organization, a Boy Scout enterprise that established itself as a small business selling books and groceries and offering to do social work around the houses of the poor. Others, like myself, wanted a clear programme of political agitation.

'You have to come out and say that, man,' James said. 'And if the rest don't agree, then smash up the whole thing.'

13

An Africa
of the Mind

One of the ideas that began James's political life in Britain was African independence. He was born into a colonial world in 1901, a world dominated by empire. In later years he used to say: 'We started agitating in the thirties for a free Africa, but if a feller had said to us that in twenty or thirty years the whole place would have thirty independent governments, we'd have expelled him as an *agent provocateur* from the Colonial Office.'

In the last decade of the twentieth century, the election of Nelson Mandela as President of South Africa put an end to the old colonial Africa. Mozambique, Angola, the Congo had all been through brutal and inter-tribal wars of independence and some of them continued to fight over the spoils, but the colonial powers had formally withdrawn.

This withdrawal from Africa was something that C.L.R. and his friends had worked towards in the 1930s through their International African Service Bureau, formed in London. In 1936 he was a founding member of the African Bureau and edited its journal, *International African Opinion*. The leading light in this enterprise was James's boyhood friend from Trinidad, Malcolm Nurse.

James's lecturing and campaigning for African independence was interrupted by his sojourn in the United States, but on his return to England he re-established contact with the African Bureau whose efforts had been overtaken by the turn of international events. The wind of change was blowing through Africa and Ghana was approaching its independence. Soon Kenya, Uganda and Tanganyika would follow.

James's first contact with Africa was Ghana. His writings may have had very little to do with Ghanaian independence, but till his last days C.L.R. James felt, justifiably or not, that he was a sort of godfather to the nation. In the end he became a disappointed one.

James had first met Kwame Nkrumah in 1941 in New York. At the time James knew him as 'Francis', Kwame's 'English' name. James became something of a mentor to the young Nkrumah. In 1943, Nkrumah told James he had enrolled to study law at University College, London, and James wrote to George Padmore asking him to make him welcome. The letter said that Nkrumah was coming down to live in England, that he was not very bright, but determined to throw the imperialists out of Africa. Recalling this letter in an essay written in 1966, James wrote: 'I am not in the least bothered at having written that Nkrumah was 'not very bright'. At the time he used to talk a great deal about imperialism, Leninism and similar data, with which my friends and I were very familiar. Nkrumah used to talk a lot of nonsense about these matters. As a matter of fact he knew nothing about them.'[1]

James was undoubtedly right. But in the next paragraph he added that Padmore, at his behest, met Nkrumah at a London railway station and thus began a friendship and a close collaboration whose main ingredient was political tutelage by Padmore of the young anti-colonial. Within a year, James says, Nkrumah had learnt a great deal and was ready to go back to Ghana and begin his political movement.

The movement succeeded and Nkrumah became the first Prime Minister of independent Ghana. In 1957, just after Ghana's independence, James went to Accra as a guest of Nkrumah. The visit was celebratory, but on his return James began, in some recess of his mind, searching for an intellectual entrance into a country of whose history he was only scantily aware.

The world was watching Ghana's development. Even months after independence the European press was looking for signs of tribal antagonisms and signs of the corruption they were convinced would engulf any independent African nation. James was on the lookout for active contributions from the African continent to the great project of proletarian and peasant activity towards a better life.

In 1960 James visited Accra again as a guest of the Government to address a convention of the ruling Party. His speech was a paean to Nkrumah and 'Nkrumahism', and curious in one particular. He told his audience that he was an advocate of a 'socialist Party' in each underdeveloped country and that the Party to which they belonged, the Convention People's Party of Ghana, was such a one.

It is curious because the James of the forties and fifties had been waging war upon the idea of a Vanguard Party and here, in one speech, he is ready to revise the doctrine for Africa.

In July 1962 he wrote to Nkrumah from Trinidad: 'Believe me, Osagyefo, more than ever in the crowded past, I am thankful and happy to know that Africa has produced so distinguished a master of the general strategy and details of the politics of humanity in the inhuman world in which we live.'

Two years later, C.L.R. would be forced to question this opinion, when the Government of Ghana was in the news. The international press pilloried it as corrupt and totalitarian. And it had good reason: there were articles about Nkrumah's palaces and about his ministers having gold taps installed in their bathrooms.

All this James chose to ignore, except when, at the end of 1963, Nkrumah dismissed his Chief Justice after a disagreement over a judgement. James wrote to Nkrumah (the letter is addressed 'Dear Francis') warning him that this interference in the independence of the judiciary was bad for Ghana and the beginning of despotism. Others were already saying that Nkrumah had proved that Africans were beginning to behave like medieval tribal chiefs and that modern government, the institutions of freedom and democracy, could never work in Africa.

In his letter James asked for an explanation. He was willing to give advice. Recollecting the affair in an essay written in 1977, James seemed to accept that Nkrumah's response amounted to a peremptory brush off. It was Prince Hal to Falstaff. He and his philosophies had become irrelevant to Nkrumah. He recalled in the essay his trips to Ghana and the conversations in which he had volunteered to write a history of Ghana's journey to independence with Nkrumah as its anti-colonial agitating hero. Nkrumah had accepted the offer. 'I told Nkrumah that it was one of the most significant revolutions of the century, and that there was still much of great importance to past and future history to be said about it. He said he had been thinking the same, and ultimately I willingly undertook to write a history of the Ghana revolution.'[2]

The book James eventually wrote was a collection of essays entitled *Nkrumah and the Ghana Revolution*, first published in 1977 (a revised edition with a new preface was published by Allison & Busby in 1982) and not the historical hagiography he had promised Nkrumah in person in 1957. The essays begin with the fall of Nkrumah rather than his rise. Other essays include an adulatory rather than deeply analytical speech which James delivered on his very brief visit from Trinidad to Accra in 1960. In fact, the motive for the book seemed to be James's determination to make public his letter of admonition to Nkrumah.

> I wrote to him at once making clear the far-reaching consequences of the mistake he had made. I asked him to write to me or ask some trusted secretary to do so. I told him that if I had been able I would have come to talk to him . . . He never replied and after a month I wrote three articles in a West Indian newspaper using the situation in Ghana as a peg on which to hang my long-felt premonitions of the African degeneration.

These later letters and the essay are, in analysis, respectful but critical. James knew that power had corrupted absolutely. And yet a substantial portion of the book is devoted to the process through the forties and fifties by which Ghana attained its independence and for this historical sequence James had only praise.

In Tanzania Dr Julius Nyerere, its first President, was beginning to formulate ideas of what he called 'African socialism'. James was respectfully interested. He would go some way in trying to understand what 'African socialism', as opposed to 'European' socialism, might be.

The result of his investigation was disappointing. James never really engaged with these African forms and traditions. His essays on them demonstrate a desperate attempt to accommodate vague ideas which he obviously recognizes as such.

Nyerere and his Government published the 'Arusha Declaration' in January 1967. In 1969 James was working on a collection of essays he intended to call *A History of Pan-African Revolt* and the preface to his chapter on Nyerere states: 'Today, the forward movement in Africa is headed along the lines of Dr Nyerere's policies.'

Nyerere had some eccentric ideas reminiscent of Gandhi's. His declaration contended that schools ought to be self-supporting farms and communities, junior kibbutzim of sorts:

> When this scheme is in operation, the revenue side of school accounts would not just read as at present—'Grant from government . . . Grant from voluntary agency or other charity . . .' They would read 'Income from the sale of cotton (or whatever other cash crop was appropriate for the area) . . . value of the food grown and consumed . . . value of labour done by pupils on new building, repairs, equipment, etc . . .'

James's approval of the scheme seems disingenuous: '. . . not in Plato or Aristotle, Rousseau or Karl Marx will you find such radical, such revolutionary departures from the established educational order'. Perhaps not in Karl Marx, but certainly in Dickens. There one finds the reality of labour forced on young children, in the name of a planned and metaphysical discipline.

James needed to find a model in Africa to which he could point as demonstrating the merger between humanism and Marxism. With hindsight, we know that the Tanzanian experiment failed but hindsight wasn't necessary to see that it was bound to fail.

The question of what concrete programmes and policies Africa must follow, however, was never C.L.R.'s primary concern. He had never studied its history in any depth and knew very little of its culture and traditions. He had never lived amongst Africans. For him, the continent was an abstract concept in which the ideas of colonialism and anti-colonialism played themselves out.

His assertions about the Western tradition he had imbibed were restricted to the West Indian and American blacks. This was mainly because he knew very little about the organization of people and production in Africa and because the little he knew told him that it was divided between subsistence economies and the vast exploitation of labour on colonial plantations and in mines.

James was wise enough not to blunder into this unknown territory with prescriptive injunctions as the movements which call themselves 'Maoist' or 'Socialist' have done. From the outset James was convinced that Africa itself must follow its own traditions and he seemed content to leave the programmes that would spring from these to the Nyereres and the Nkrumahs, the actual rulers in Africa.

This wasn't a sudden modesty on the part of the intellectual who had advocated whole programmes of world revolution. It was quite plain to him that in Africa he was making judgements without the sort of detailed reading and assessment he had devoted to Russia or America.

In the thirties, when C.L.R. first began to write about Africa and to agitate for military aid to Ethiopia, the agenda was not development but decolonization. Now the heirs of that decolonization had to grasp the nettle of government.

· · ·

James's other brush with Africa came when he refused to go to the
sixth Pan-African Congress in 1974. James had been instrumental
in calling for the conference. Several American and West Indian
politicians and intellectuals approached him to become a sponsor
of the conference and lend his name to a revival of Pan-Africanism.

The conference took months to plan. It was to be a meeting of
the newly independent black states around the world and to culmi-
nate in a Pan-Africanist philosophy. The very concept of the conference was flawed, as James realized when the committee organizing
it attempted to include the opposition parties in each country. The
invitees would be divided into the governments, who were for the
most part being denounced by their leftist and Marxist opposition
parties as collaborators and neo-colonialists, and these denouncers
themselves. Realizing this, the invited governments began to make
conditions. When opposition delegates were refused guest status,
they complained to James, who alerted other delegates, asking them
to boycott the conference. When Nyerere himself put in a call to
James, then at Howard University, asking him to change his mind,
James declined. He didn't attend the congress and the opposition
parties were kept out but when it took place they and their supporters staged protests which were reported in the press.

A reader of James's essays on Africa will learn very little of the
geography, history or people of Africa: 'The future of Africa will be
rooted in the African experience of African life. Yet nobody, European or African, can make anything clear or consistent of the developing pattern in Africa unless upon the basis of the substantially
documented and widely debated historical experiences of Western
civilization.'[3]

James's 1977 collection of essays on Africa, in which his assessment of the Arusha Declaration is reproduced, included an essay on
Lenin and the question of who does what in a revolution. He re-
examined Lenin's view of the tasks that lay before Russia and the
Bolshevik Party after the seizure of power. From Lenin's last essays

James isolated two: 'On education' and 'The workers and peasants inspection'.

In going back to Lenin, James was drawing implicit lessons for Ghana, other African states and the West Indies. It was an attempt to look at Nkrumah's mistakes obliquely, through a Leninist lesson.

James summed up Lenin's prescriptions in two points. The first was education. Teach the peasantry literacy, numeracy, history, culture, skills. The second was the overhaul of the apparatus of government, including the Party itself. Lenin believed that having inherited the tsarist state, the Bolsheviks must break it up and rebuild it. The control of the party must pass from a bureaucracy to the people, and for this purpose Lenin proposed the mobilization of a large pseudo-parliamentary body. He called it an inspection because it was to approve or veto the actions of government.

For Lenin, James hoped people would read 'C.L.R.'. And for tsarist, they might substitute 'colonial'.

For whom was he now writing? His audience was no longer the activists of a small movement. It was no longer the movers and shakers of an anti-colonial caucus. James had reassumed the role of writer. Trinidad had disappointed him by not conforming to the abstracts. His attempts at practical political intervention had been spectacular failures. In his mind, in the sixties, he still hoped that a younger generation in Ghana, in Africa, would begin to understand his words and steer their countries his way.

14

His Name in Vain

Throughout his life C.L.R. James wrote about and anticipated the revolt of the black populations of the United States and the Caribbean. His prediction of them, and indeed his guidance of some of the brains behind the smaller agitations and upheavals in the Caribbean, gave him the distinction of being a parent or grandparent of the upheavals.

Very few prophets live to see their prophecies come true. But the irony, which would not have escaped C.L.R. James, was that the form that several of these revolts took in the Caribbean was tragic and cruel. They ended in murder and mayhem and not in the liberation and hope that his Marxist formulations had predicted.

The tragedy that befell Grenada in the late seventies and early eighties has been traced back, in some cases by writers with a limited understanding of the situation, to the political influence of C.L.R. James. It is the fate of many a prophet: the word is twisted, the inspiration distorted into its opposite. What began in Grenada as a 'revolution' ended in tragic murder, revolutionary against revolutionary.

In 1979 a party, led by a small group of London-trained lawyers, schoolteachers and self-proclaimed revolutionaries, stood for parliament in Grenada. The New Jewel Movement, which had come about as the result of the amalgamation of tiny groups in Grenada, one of which had connections with the 'Jamesian' group called New Beginnings in Trinidad, was defeated in the election. The leaders of this party, who had mounted a vigorous campaign towards the election, were not satisfied with being a loyal opposition. Though they had stood for elections, they didn't believe in 'bourgeois democracy' and were unwilling to play the game.

Their campaign for election had gone further than criticize the ruling Party of Prime Minister Eric Gairy. It had denounced this Government as the corrupt lackeys of American interests who would sell the resources and the population back into slavery. Having taken this stance, they couldn't revert completely to being a loyal opposition and voting futilely in the lobbies.

The leaders of the New Jewel Movement waited for Eric Gairy, their eccentric Prime Minister, to leave the country to attend a conference of UFO-spotters in Miami and staged a coup d'état. They marched on the police station, which surrendered without a shot, and then occupied Government buildings and offices.

They displaced the tin-pot Prime Minister and his Government and declared a revolutionary regime. Soon after the coup the revolutionaries, who had suspended the parliament, began looking for ways in which they could implement a 'socialist' programme.

Maurice Bishop, who became Prime Minister after the coup, had picked up on the works of James through New Beginnings. A London-trained lawyer, he now found himself the unlikely Prime Minister of a tiny country and the leader of its revolution and he sought C.L.R.'s advice by coming to see him in London. The meeting was not minuted and its proceedings were kept very secret but a few years after it, when events took a tragic turn on the island, C.L.R. told me that he had warned Bishop about communist influence and subversion in his Government and told him that there was no possibility of any 'socialist' pattern of society emerging in an island as tiny and as unindustrialized as Grenada. All he could and must give the people of Grenada was 'good government'. It was a phrase he often used.

Whether Maurice Bishop took any note of his advice one can never know. He returned to Grenada and faced several problems. There was no investment in the island. The fishermen were unhappy with having no refrigeration facility, the nutmeg farmers wanted to hike their prices.

The island economy was soon in trouble and the rhetoric that the New Jewel Movement had adopted—calling each other 'comrade' was the least of it—made the Americans and potential investors from Europe suspicious. The Party had no way of solving the practical problems of the population and the leaders began to tell the rank and file members that they had to be vigilant and guard against American subversion, which was everywhere.

The Party began to assume the identity of a secret organization. The minutes of its meetings and gatherings began to be couched in an absurd Leninist rhetoric and jargon, referring to the tiny population of the island as the 'broad masses' and to anyone who criticized them as 'reactionaries' and 'agents'. Government had become a carnival as they slipped into the costumes and the argot of Bolshevism.

But the masquerade turned deadly. Factions within the New Jewel Movement fought over the leadership, disguising the fight in obscure 'Leninist' rhetoric as a matter of principle and direction. They were soon at each other's throats.

Within four years the island's economy, such as it was, was in crisis. The Deputy Prime Minister, one Bernard Coard, a trained mining engineer and Bishop's comrade and friend, was in charge of the economy. He sought the help of Cuba. Fidel Castro responded favourably. Tiny though it was, here was a potential ally and a sister communist nation in the Caribbean. He would give them aid, training and what's more he would build a new airport for them.

Members of the New Jewel Movement got in touch with James in London, where he was living in the early eighties. He was deeply distrustful of their propaganda and the Party's newspaper. It was couched, he said, in Stalinist rhetoric.

The New Jewel Movement government invited him to the island.

'You think I want to go there? I will go nowhere near there. They do this and that in my name but these fellers are Stalinists, they will kill me,' he said to me.

He was deeply cynical about the role of Bernard Coard and his wife Phyllis who was Jamaican by birth and the heiress of the family that owned the Tia Maria liqueur brand. About Maurice Bishop he was kinder. He said the fellow meant well.

He was right. In 1983 the Government of Grenada split into warring factions. Bernard Coard put Maurice Bishop under house arrest and declared him to be an agent of imperialism and an enemy of the state. Coard was in control of a small Cuban-trained military with Russian armoured cars imported from Cuba.

His arrest of Bishop misfired. 'The broad masses', or a few hundred people, went to the house where Maurice Bishop and his girlfriend, the Education Minister Jackie Creft, were being held prisoner by the Coards. The crowd managed to persuade the guards to set free the Prime Minister and the Education Minister, who hadn't eaten for four days. They then carried them jubilantly up the hill to the old fort, one of the vantage points of the port capital, St Georges.

From another vantage point on the island where he had made his revolutionary headquarters, Coard sent his armoured cars after Bishop, Creft and their remaining friends. The armoured cars went up the hill to the old fort and demanded, in the name of the revolution, the surrender of Bishop and his reactionary agents. Bishop, it is reported, surrendered but an enthusiastic commander of the revolutionary forces wouldn't accept the surrender. He lined up nine members of the Bishop faction, including Bishop and Creft, who was pregnant with his child, and shot them.

The armoured cars then proceeded to shoot into the crowd and hundreds of people died in the slaughter, of bullet wounds and through trying to jump off the cliffs of the fort to get away from the firing. The island couldn't absorb this trauma and tragedy. The American marines were sent in to secure the peace by Ronald Reagan who, it is reputed, had to ask White House staff, 'Where the hell is Grenada?'

The American marines restored some sort of order and the Cuban workers building the new airport were arrested and sent home. Bernard and Phyllis Coard and their supporters were rounded up and subsequently tried for murder.

Fidel Castro himself turned against the murderers.

At the beginning of this tragic farce, the revolutionaries declared that they were 'Jamesians' and that this was the first real revolution inspired by the ideas of C.L.R. James, just as the ideas of Lenin had guided the events in St Petersburg in 1917.

No other revolution directly traced its roots to James's inspiration and James denounced this one that claimed it did. Still, there was no doubt that several of the post-independence politicians in the Caribbean islands had been reared on the thoughts and books of C.L.R. James. One who acknowledged his debt to James was Walter Rodney who led a militant agitation in Guyana against the then Prime Minister, Forbes Burnham, before dying mysteriously in a car bomb attack.

As the only eminent Marxist theoretician the Caribbean has produced, it is tempting to lay every tragedy of the sad islands at James's door—or if not at his door, at the imaginative threshold of the many mansions he built.

On my visit to Grenada in 1995, which I have already described in Chapter 11, I met Bernard Coard, whom I had known in London when we were both schoolteachers. The new Government of Grenada of the nineties had given us access to him, now in prison on Richmond Hill, his death sentence having been commuted to life imprisonment.

In the early seventies, Coard, living and teaching in Britain, wrote a pamphlet accusing the British school system of systematically destroying the black identity of West Indian children. It caused comment in the newspapers for a day and in teaching circles for a few months. Then Bernard Coard dropped out of sight. A few years later I read in the papers that he was part of the movement in Grenada which had taken revolutionary charge of the island. James had always said he distrusted Coard, but during our visit he was unambiguous about the fact the 'the movement' had been inspired by the revolutionary writings of James.

Perhaps it is inevitable that a man of Caribbean origin who spends his life writing about world revolution will find disciples amongst Caribbean people. But the tragedy of James is that his concern was a philosophy of world revolution, lofty ideas that didn't connect with the political consequences of managing an economy that subsisted on nutmeg. James had reached beyond the social and intellectual horizons of the Caribbean.

It was inevitable that the pretenders of Grenada would look for a West Indian mentor. James was invited by the New Jewel three times and, like Julius Caesar, declined the crown of Grenada on all three occasions. He thought they were fools playing with fire.

15

Your Move, Hungarian

It started with a phone call from Darcus Howe. Darcus and I had been friends for fifteen years. We had been through the Black Power movement of Britain as agitators, pamphleteers, cronies.

Darcus was C.L.R. James's grand nephew. He phoned to ask if James could live in my house for a few days. I had a spare room and he needed a place. I was flattered to be asked and went in my car to fetch the old man.

James was polite and took me entirely for granted. I was a man of political convictions; I had read his books; I said I had met him before though I doubt if he remembered; I was a friend of his grand nephew's. And that was that. He would accept my hospitality.

I knew that this would entail receiving his visitors and taking his phone calls, making his meals and doing his laundry. That was fine with me. I didn't have a nine to five job as I'd quit being a school-teacher and was now writing scripts and books.

We got on well. We talked about books and art and writers and plays and poets, Marx and Lenin, Beethoven and Mozart, claret and Confucius, cabbages and kings.

He was prodigiously curious. He would ask questions, detailed questions of everyone who passed through the flat, my friends and associates, visitors, journalists, anyone.

A lady called Marushka came by appointment to visit James. She told me that she was doing research of some sort but I have forgotten now what it was. He was very welcoming and, sitting up on the bed in his room in the house, fully dressed, he asked her to sit in a chair by him. He proceeded to debrief her. Very thoroughly. His questions were always verging on the pedantic.

'No, tell me again. You go out of your house at about eight o'clock, fine. Then where do you go?'

'To the tube.'

'Ah. The tube and there are a lot of people about?'

'Yes, packed out at that time. The rush hour.'

'I see. And you get to your destination, a library, an hour later?'

Routines. He wanted to know her routines. I left them alone. I had meetings.

When I returned that evening they were both still there, in the same positions, frozen as if in a game. She said she had made some coffee and hoped I didn't mind and James said he had instructed her to go out and buy 'those bread things with holes in them'.

'Crumpets.' I prompted.

'Yes, but this is a fine lady,' he said to me in her presence. 'She speaks five languages, knows music and culture. We shall go to the opera together. She is remarkably well read. A woman of great distinction. She has read several of my books, man!'

Marushka came back the next day and the next.

'Open some claret, man,' C.L.R. would say.

Then, when she didn't come for two days he began to agitate and fret.

'Will you call her, man. I have told her I can make sense of what she is writing about: the Second World War and the West Indians who fought in it. I knew several of them. I can go through my old diaries and find them. But she has to have a position on that.'

I didn't call her. She came back by herself a few days later. Again they talked for hours.

Once I entered the room and caught them holding hands. He was eighty. She was probably around thirty.

When she was with him, James treated the subject of West Indians in the wars as though Lenin himself had sanctioned its importance. The old man had thought up a theory for Marushka. She filled his days over the next few weeks as nothing else did.

Before Marushka's appearance, James and I would set off in my rickety car and, at the old man's tyrannical behest, look for a Chinese restaurant that was open at three in the afternoon. We would eat, drink, talk and come home.

After the coming of Marushka, he said he'd like to invite her to lunch and I was to drive. We waited for her arrival, but he had the dates wrong and we set out on our own after waiting an hour. We used to eat at an Italian restaurant in Soho to which he'd taken a shine. We patronized it and made friends with the maître d' who would seat us and serve us as old friends. That day, sullen through disappointment at having got the day or time of the appointment with Marushka wrong, C.L.R. said he would like to examine the bill. He insisted that I add it up and look at the menu to check the prices, something we hadn't done in our months of confident patronage.

Sure enough, the bill was wrong. Several pounds had been added to it. I pointed it out to the maître d' and the bill was instantly changed, a profound apology proffered and a round of brandy offered—on the house. The old man became silent. As we walked out to the car I asked him how he knew that we were being swindled.

'I liked talking to that man,' was his reply. 'It was fortunate she didn't come, man. These episodes are humiliating.'

After that day we tried other restaurants and found none the old man wished to adopt. Once, with the rain pouring down and Nello wearing his broad-brimmed hat and his long navy coat, we were refused admittance to a busy Italian restaurant in Soho. There were empty tables but the man at the door, wearing an apron and with bulging eyeballs, said sorry we couldn't go in. He was looking C.L.R. up and down.

'I don't want to go there,' James said, with extreme insistence. 'Let's just go.'

'I think we should insist. Bastards!' I said. I didn't want to turn my back on it. I knew I'd feel a fool later. I was staring at the young Italian.

'I said no,' said the old man.

I gave way and we went. We ate a Chinese meal. We talked briefly about Marushka who seemed to have disappeared altogether.

A few weeks later she came back. The old man had clearly been hoping she would because, though he never mentioned her, his delight was obvious. She was effusive towards him, as though they had known each other a long time. He asked me to leave as she sat down at the foot of his bed.

What do I make of this? That attractive women are impressed by intellect? 'Age no bar?' as they say in the desperate matrimonial ads columns of Indian newspapers. Possibly.

He played her his favourite records and talked about what each composer was trying to achieve. She phoned the next day to ask if it was convenient to visit. He said he had been waiting for her. Once he put the phone down, he asked for an Afro comb to push back his shock of full white hair. He was dressed in blue jeans and a coloured shirt which he chose carefully from those I'd ironed.

Before she left him this time, there was an invitation. He had written the address down, and she had written it again on the same sheet of paper. Parliament Hill, north London.

Lunch at her place. He had asked her whether she would cook for him and she said she probably would. The date was for Saturday. Today was Tuesday.

Three difficult days. He talked of the books he had lent her and of her thesis that he would read for her. Perhaps I would, as she had asked, see my way to promoting a TV programme about the West Indians in the RAF?

On Friday night we went through a drill. A bath, then an examination of the ironed shirts. The tickets for the dry-cleaning had been lost. Like the ugly sisters going to the ball, we blamed each other.

'So you will drop me and you will pick me up, man. I'll tell you the time when we get there.'

In good time on Saturday we drove out. The old man was wearing his broad-brimmed hat. He had insisted on wearing a suit. We bought a bottle of wine on the way. 'A Médoc,' he specified.

The house was in a street which the council had sequestered from traffic on behalf of the upper middle-class residents. I helped the old man out of the car and we found the house.

My instructions said the basement so we descended the stairs. A young black man answered the bell.

'Marushka?' I said.

'Yes, yes, come, come, come,' he said, stepping aside flamboyantly. The old man's face flickered from mellow expectation to alert observation.

The basement was open-plan. There were ten or twelve people there. A tall handsome black man made his way across the room and grabbed James with both hands.

'Nello, man. So happy to see you. How are you?'

'I am getting on, you know.' The champion was annoyed. No Marushka.

I stood around and the man, apparently the host, introduced himself to me. He and the old man were already well acquainted, more than friends.

'I'm George Lamming. Hello. Come in, have a drink.'

Lamming! The famous writer on whom the old man had written essays.

I sat the old man down as Marushka came down a stairway at the back. She went up to the old man and kissed him on the cheek. Then she got into some conversation with Lamming which seemed to imply that they were co-hosts of this party. She had called her people and he had called his and they had mutual friends. All very cosy. The old man was thrown.

There were six or seven black people there who knew who C.L.R. James was. I had been instructed ten times to leave as soon as I got him there and I had made commitments.

'All right, C.L.R., I'll see you later. Tell me what time.'

'You can't leave me, man. Don't you see what's going on here?'

'No, I don't,' I said.

I tackled Marushka. 'The old man didn't know it was going to be a party, and that Lamming was going to be here?'

'It's George's house,' she said. 'I live here.' She pointed upstairs.

'So what time shall I come back and pick him up?'

By now the old man was being given a drink and people were gathering round him to talk. Business as usual. I stalked out of the basement, carrying the burden of his disappointment and finding it absurd.

Three or four hours later I returned. The basement was quiet. The old man was sitting by himself. He had run out of conversation.

'Where have you been?' he demanded. 'You abandoned me here. Let's go, let's just go. I wanted to leave from the moment I came in, but you just left me, man.'

As we went out I rubbed it in. 'So she lives in Lamming's house? You know Lamming from way back, don't you? She never told you?'

'I want nothing to do with these people, man, I know them well.'

On the ride back to south London and up the stairs to his room, the old man kept a resolute silence. As far as I knew, Marushka didn't call again.

16

Black Power
and After

The ultimate irony of James's life was that he was brought to prominence by a movement he predicted but couldn't intellectually support.

'I'm getting off this bandwagon, thanks for the ride' could or should have been his final slogan. But he maintained a dignified silence, partly perhaps because he didn't want to poop the party, and partly because the direction that black power took had racial connotations and developments with which James could have no truck. He had worked all his life before black power was born, with whites and with Jews. They had been his comrades, companions and personal friends. With them, he had advocated the cause of black autonomy within the American left movement and with them he had tried to raise black American opposition to the Second World War.

James was not to know that this politically principled black opposition to war would not take active shape in that war but would turn the United States upside down in a subsequent one. He was not to know that black opposition to the Vietnam War would even become a powerful factor in the defeat of the United States.

James was living in Britain when the Vietnam War brought America to this point of internal revolt. Black Civil Rights leaders, and millions of their followers, forcefully expressed their opposition to the Vietnam War and successive Presidents of the US could not ignore them.

As James had done during the Second World War, Martin Luther King and his followers linked the lack of rights at home to the injustice of conscription. But the success of the Vietnam protests encouraged further demands. Martin Luther King's non-violent campaign came up against other organizations which articulated the idea that if non-violence didn't work violence might.

At the beginning of the Black Power movement, Stokely Carmichael coined the slogan or, as James preferred to put it, raised the banner of, 'Black Power'. When Carmichael came to London in 1967, it was abuzz with the new idea. It was the era of soft revolt, the haircuts and the Beatles, the leather jackets and the Rolling Stones. The notion of Black Power turned it into an era of hard revolt.

At a political jamboree in 1968 at a converted railway shed called the Round House in Chalk Farm in London, both Stokely Carmichael and James were invited to speak. The conference was a public three-day affair and was, typically for the flamboyant sixties, called 'The Dialectics of Liberation and the Demystification of Violence'.

Stokely Carmichael spoke for forty minutes. His key phrase throughout was 'it is crystal clear to me . . .' What was clear to him was that the black population of the United States was oppressed, was in revolt and had the right to fight back. James openly disagreed. Not with these points at all but with the idea that blacks were alone. To loud applause, almost as loud as the applause Stokely received for his aggressive assertions, he affirmed his faith in a broad multiracial alliance of forces in America.

The idea and slogan of Black Power began to spread in Britain. It was a powerful phrase. Power hadn't been given a colour before, but the phrase was plangent with meanings, some of them rallying, some threatening.

James was asked to address a private audience of black and white activists of various allegiances on the subject of Black Power. This was something that the immigrants to Britain from the West Indies, Africa, India and Pakistan hadn't adopted yet, though there had been for at least ten years a vibrant immigrant rights movement. James began by praising the young Stokely Carmichael. He traced the history of Negro ideological thought from Booker T. Washington, through W. E. B. Du Bois to Stokely Carmichael. What he didn't say was that he himself, in his view on autonomous Negro struggles presented to Trotsky in 1939, had predicted such a movement and welcomed it.

All his life, James had written, lectured and battled against nationalism. Yet now, when blacks moved to form their own militant organizations with eccentric ideologies, James decided that this was the movement he had been talking about. In his speech he welcomed the Black Power movement. Here were the Negro masses projecting their own leadership without the assistance of a party.

At last the black nationalist genie had escaped from the lamp.

But James had to be the master of the genie, not its slave. He was sure of one thing, which was that a whole population rather than a small group would reach a point of dissatisfaction which would be decisive. The revolt of the blacks of America or elsewhere was a subcategory of this idea and James didn't want the Black Power and, subsequently, the black studies advocates to hijack the larger idea.

He could clearly see the dangers that this hijacking would lead to, and his fears were borne out. People jumped on the bandwagon. Nixon in his political campaigns, for example, merrily endorsed 'black capitalism'. He argued that the black populations of the USA should be encouraged to set up their own production bases and cater in some measure to black markets. This was a form of black autonomy favoured by the Black Muslim movements such as the Nation of Islam, but it wasn't a direction that James advocated or sanctioned.

James saw the complex phenomenon of black revolt in the seventies through the prism of his conviction. He had for many years believed that the United States would be the society of the future and its movements must herald that dawn, and he saw the black movement in the United States take huge strides and transform the social and political balance of the country. The history of the transformation, the gains made by the Civil Rights movements has yet to be written. James, living in Britain and lecturing in the United States, was acutely aware that this great current of transformation carried within it the flotsam and jetsam, the debris of severe prejudice, superstition, cultist ideology and reaction.

Even so, the moment he had been talking about to Trotsky in 1939 had come, and had even revived a demand for his work. But the moment could turn awkward and no one was more aware of this than James. In a lecture in London on Black Power, published subsequently by the Marcus Garvey Institute in the USA, James says he is setting out to clarify a concept 'which means so many different things to so many different people'.

I want to take in particular Mr Rap Brown, who makes the most challenging statements, is prepared to challenge American racial prejudice to the utmost limit of his strength and the strength of the Negroes who will follow him. Who are we to say, 'Yes, you are entitled to say this but not to say that; you are entitled to do this but not to do that'?

What Brown is doing is this: he is taking care that the total rejection of second-class citizenship, the single-mindedness, the determination to fight to death if need be, which now permeates the Negro movement, will not be corrupted, modified or in any way twisted from its all-embracing purpose by white do-gooders and well-wishers of whom the United States is full.

Racism is on the decline in the United States. Yes, on the decline. Years ago you used to have white people fighting against black people. Not today . . . What is taking place

in American city after American city is black people fighting against the police. In other words, they are challenging
an ancient enemy which is one wing of the state power.
That is not racism, that is revolutionary politics.[1]

The paradox inherent in Jamesian thinking is that nothing that
James said or did in his years in the United States contributed to this
awakening. As far as Black Power was concerned it came about
without James. And yet it arrived as he predicted that it would,
unprompted by ideologues, and this was what he saw as most significant. He was called upon, of course, but only when it had established itself as a phenomenon and began grappling for direction. By
the time he began lecturing in the US in the early seventies, the
black movement and its military organizations had been infiltrated
by the FBI and destroyed by infighting.

A long-standing collaborator with James, Martin Glaberman,
the chairman of the Correspondence Group that emerged from the
splits of the Johnson–Forest Tendency in the 1940s, wrote to James
in the sixties to ask for advice on these ideas of blacks and revolution. James's reply was strident, rejecting Glaberman's assertion
that the black movement could or should be insulated from all criticism:

In the paragraph before the last you said, 'What we all
have to understand is that the policies of Negro organizations do not have to pass muster with anyone but the
masses of Negroes themselves.'

That is simply not true. A massive movement like the
Negro movement is bound to consider the effect of whatever it says upon others besides Negroes . . .

You go on to say, 'No one else has any right to stand in
judgement.'

That is simply untrue. Everyone has every right to stand
in judgement.[2]

The Black Panthers had asserted their right to carry guns, a theatrical gesture rather than a serious terrorist threat. The Panthers walked tall on the streets, with black berets and guns to demonstrate that militancy could rise in the ranks of the black population. But blacks in the USA had no tradition of the kind of disciplined secrecy essential to the organization of terrorism.

Parallel to them there arose the religious nationalism of Elijah Muhammad and the Nation of Islam. Founded by a door-to-door salesman called Wallace D. Farad, who mysteriously disappeared in 1934, the sect set up a Temple of Islam in reaction to the domination of America by dissenting Christians. Elijah Muhammad, who was born Elijah Poole, took control of the Temple and, calling himself a messenger of Allah, imposed a strict moral code on its followers, amongst them Malcolm X.

Born Malcolm Little, Malcolm X began his adult life in the company of thieves, pimps and drug peddlers. In his autobiography he charted his transformation through the disciplining force of Islam. Praying five times a day and abandoning drink, drugs, whoring and crime were discipline enough.

Following the injunction of Islam he went on a pilgrimage to Mecca, a *Hajj,* the Muslim's dutiful journey to the shrine of the prophet. There he met Muslims of all colours and races and the encounter engendered doubts about the racial preachings of his mentor Elijah who heretically maintained that he was a prophet.

Malcolm X came to believe that Islam as preached by the Nation of Islam was not only sacrilegious and the deepest blasphemy but was also a farrago of racial nonsense. America had produced a religion devoted to race hatred in reverse and Elijah had labelled it Islam. He now saw that it provided only obscure and obscurantist answers to the problems of injustice in US society.

Malcolm broke with the Nation and set out on his own to stimulate an active mass movement of blacks which would take action at the point of grievance. The Nation sent their assassins to shoot him.

All James's learning and all his wit couldn't prevent the animus of the black movements from being virulently 'nationalistic', as it became under Malcolm and his former mentor, Elijah. In other words, the impulse that animated the black masses wasn't inspired by Marx. It was animated by resentment and orchestrated by a sense of drama, with the rhetoric of black church sermons in support.

This was not James's inspiration and neither was the idea of 'black studies' for which there began to be a clamour, once the idea of 'black' as a new nationalist identity filtered into the academies and the demands of the black movement were transformed from the material to the theoretical. These studies in turn yielded lists and achievements of black heroes, 'achievers', 'icons' and 'role models'.

James's name appeared on these registered as an intellectual heavyweight, together with those of Marcus Garvey, W. E. B. Du Bois, slaves who had run away in Elizabethan times, a black nurse from the Crimean War, a man who had invented traffic lights and other people whose graves should have been left undisturbed by bounty hunters.

C.L.R. James did not belong in this company but the head-hunters of black studies dragged him into their demi-world and his meticulous life's work onto shelves filled with unsaleable books of black cartoons. Through the seventies, as this movement for black studies grew and James's name was bandied about by a new generation that hadn't read his works, he supported the idea but not the ideas of Black Power. In 1969, in a lecture reproduced in his collected essays he was still saying, 'I do not recognize any distinctive nature of black studies—not today in 1969. This is the history of black people and white people and all serious students of modern history have to know. To say it's some kind of ethnic problem is a lot of nonsense.'[3]

It's an undeserved fate, but one that James had to face towards the end of his life. Black Power made him famous. Black nationalism promoted his fame while not understanding that he stood against their notions.

. . .

In 1974 James retired from his post at Howard University and returned to Britain. He had acquired a new pre-eminence, a paradoxical one in many ways, but he hadn't acquired a home. The marriage to Selma had broken up.

The relationship came under severe strain owing to the constant lack of money, and, after frequent separation during their life together, James left for ever. There was an acrimonious divorce in the eighties about which James would say very little.

Their last years together were bitter. Selma, a political figure in her own right, had assembled around her a handful of women in a group called the Wages For Housework Collective. It was not, according to C.L.R. James, a serious political movement, or indeed a perspective which greatly concerned him. He treated the movement with amused disdain and once, in my presence, with impatient irritation. He wanted no more arguments about Wages For Housework or Wages Due Lesbians, an offshoot of the same group.

When I challenged him on these matters he said with some finality, 'They must be left to do what they want to do. They argue about who does the cooking. Those who will cook will cook, those who won't cook, won't cook.'

The personal tensions between C.L.R. and Selma were disguised as political disagreement. C.L.R. called his grand nephew. He couldn't stay in the house any longer, and, after the short while as my guest, he moved into the flat above the offices of *Race Today*, the black radical magazine edited by Darcus Howe.

The room, corridor, kitchen and bathroom of the *Race Today* flat were on the second floor of a squat-turned-licensee premise on the corner of Railton Road and Shakespeare Road in Brixton, south London. Brixton is sometimes called the Harlem of London and was for several decades from the late sixties to the nineties a predominantly black area. Very occasionally, C.L.R. would be helped down the two flights of stairs and taken out in a car. He was mostly content to stay in his room, almost always content to stay in bed.

At that time, in his eighties, James attracted a new group of followers, a handful of white devotees and black academic students, who grew as the years went by into black academics more concerned with academe than community. They were bookish people, dedicated to the academic pursuit of theories of revolt. James had supplied such theories and his works were ideal for such study. Some were and are serious academics, others merely sought pro-black credentials.

It is August 1981. Nello is living with me and I am to drive him down to the Riverside Studios, a theatre and cultural centre in west London, where he is to lecture on the emergence of three black women writers in America. He is championing Toni Morrison after the publication of her very first novel, long before she becomes a candidate for America's glittering prizes. The second writer he has chosen is Alice Walker, again a considerable time before Steven Spielberg adopts her novel *The Color Purple* and makes her an internationally known writer. The third is a poet called Ntozake Shange, an African-American whose work at the time was little known.

He spends a few days writing notes for his lecture, mostly in the margins of the books he goes through over and over again. He refuses to discuss the substance of his lecture with me, though he tells me the gist of his thesis. It is not profound, but staggering in its simplicity. Black women who have been scrubbing and cleaning and on their knees or backs for centuries are now, with this representation, at the forefront of American literature.

He carries the books with him when we set out. He wears his large broad-brimmed American hat, his features gaunt beneath it. He insists on his blue suit, now shiny with ironing. I have polished his shoes.

We get to the Riverside and he is received like royalty. We are taken to a Green Room to wait. The foyer and the café area through which the artists and the audience enter is packed with chattering black and white people, like a theatre audience, expectant and respectful.

When we get to the Green Room, Nello tells me he wants to sit in peace for a few minutes without any disturbance whatsoever. He needs to gather his thoughts and mark the pages to which he will refer. If the management has any queries about microphones and cups of tea they are to ask me.

I leave him in the Green Room and am taken for a few moments by the conscientious technicians of the centre to the hall as it fills up. When I get back, the door of the Green Room is ajar. A very grumpy, scowling and silent Nello is sitting in an easy chair and around him are six or seven people.

'What's going on?' I ask.

A distraught young white man, an attendant at the theatre stands near the door. 'I told them they couldn't come in, but they just pushed past. Now please . . .'

'I told you not to leave me, man!' is all Nello will say. He points to me. 'You ask him any questions.'

At the centre of the circle is a very light skinned old lady with a turban and a gown. With her is a gentleman. He too wears a turban with a large precious stone or glass bead pinned to its front. These smiling personages are obviously the stars of this group. With them are three young black women. One of them steps forward.

'Are you Mr James's attendant?'

'I suppose I am. Now can you leave? He really needs a few moments on his own.'

'We've come to the lecture, just to see Mr James. This is Queen Mother Moore.'

The old lady smiles. 'We are very old friends,' she says.

I look at Nello, but he is stoney-faced and gazing into the distance.

I usher the party out, muttering that they will meet him after the lecture. Then it's time to go.

The theatre is packed. I escort C.L.R. to the stage and sit him down. I notice that the theatrically dressed couple and their acolytes have taken seats in the upper back rows. The lecture is engaging and successful. The audience is asked to put their questions about the writers C.L.R. has been discussing. They move on to the broader concerns of literature and its effects on politics.

Then the gentleman with Queen Mother Moore indicates that he would like to ask a question. He gets to his feet at the chairman's indication and asks Nello what he is going to do about the dollars, the plot of land and the donkey that the United States' President Abraham Lincoln promised all the freed slaves of the USA. These reparations were promised, were never delivered, are long overdue and he is determined to see that the debt is paid.

The audience doesn't know how to respond to this question. Is this the height of revolutionary consciousness, delivered by a gentleman who is dressed like Ali Baba out of some pantomime? Nello decides it's pantomime. His reply is impatient and contemptuous.

'I came here to speak about literature and some important writers. I know nothing about donkeys but if you want them I hope you get them,' he says.

After the session he doesn't want to go back to the Green Room and asks me if I can find a back door that will take us out to the car and away.

The next day the phone rings incessantly. The young lady at the other end is insistent. They have tracked my phone number down and want to make an appointment for Queen Mother Moore with Nello. Nello listens while I take the calls and shakes his finger. I make an excuse as to why I can't make the appointment or disclose my address.

'These are dangerous people, keep them away, I tell you,' he says.

'They seemed perfectly harmless, masquerade-wallahs,' I say, playing Watson to Sherlock Holmes.

'You have no idea. If they catch up with you, they cling to you, like a burr.'

They phone again and I've run out of excuses.

'He can't still be asleep. You're holding out on me,' says a female voice with an American accent.

'Tell them anything, man,' Nello indiscreetly prompts from the other room. 'Tell them C.L.R. James is dead, he died this afternoon.'

I do as I am told. I say C.L.R. has died suddenly. A long silence. The caller is consulting someone.

'When is the funeral?'

'I can't say,' I say. 'It was all very sudden and his nephew Darcus Howe has taken the body off to a secret location in the Caribbean.'

This is too much for them. The phone is banged down. Nello says nothing about it for a few hours. Then he chuckles to himself. 'That's it. C.L.R. is dead. Dead as a doorknob. We have them on the run, boys!'

When I was offered a job, I asked Nello what I should do. Even though he'd moved out of my house, I used to see him regularly. I had been writing for a living; books, a drama series for the BBC, a comedy series for Channel 4, and now I had been offered full-time employment in Channel 4 as the commissioning editor for multicultural programmes.

For me it was a challenge. If I took the job I would determine part of what appeared on the Channel 4 screens. The radical part. The life and imagination, the history and preoccupations of the new populations of Britain, the Indians, Pakistanis, Africans, Bangladeshis, West Indians, Chinese, still had to be brought to television. Without a moment's hesitation he said 'take it'.

We had worked together for Channel 4. The previous commissioner of multicultural programming, Sue Woodford, whose father was Trinidadian, had sought out James when he was living with me and asked him if he would do a series of lectures for the new channel.

James agreed. The lectures were to be prerecorded in front of invited audiences. They were to last for half an hour and James could choose the subjects. I would help him with his research, iron his shirts and see that he got taxis to the venues on time.

James chose as his six subjects: Pan-Africanism, Shakespeare, Solidarity and the Polish Revolt, American Politics, the West Indies, and Cricket.

Preparation posed no problem. He was like a schoolboy who had won all the trophies on prize day. He boasted to everyone who came to the house that he had been asked by Channel 4 to 'tell them what James thinks'.

The lectures were—and still are—remarkable. Jeremy Isaacs, the Chief Executive of Channel 4 at the time, a veteran of TV and a pioneer of the radical voice on the screen, nominated the James lectures when he retired from the post as among the ten best things for which he had been responsible.

But the lecture that stood out was James's discourse on the Solidarnosc (Solidarity) movement in Poland. At the time, the workers of the Gdansk shipyard, one of the country's cardinal industries in the north, were in full revolt. An industrial strike of discontented workers had escalated into a revolt against Poland's puppet Government and against Russian colonization.

James contended that Solidarity, the unofficial organization of workers in Poland, was the new 'universal', a form of getting together which would be the vehicle of revolution.

He was right. Solidarity did succeed in overthrowing the Polish regime. Its existence began the stand-off between Russia and its rebellious satellites which ended with Russia declaring that the people of Poland, East Germany, Hungary, Rumania and the rest could do what they wanted with their governments. It was the beginning of the end for these puppet regimes and the beginning of the end of the Soviet empire.

What James said in a lecture on Channel 4 in July 1983 was that the revolt that began in Gdansk 'would end in Leningrad and Moscow'.

James didn't live to see its complete overthrow, but what he fervently predicted in 1984 came to pass a few years later.

. . .

The difficulty, the obscurity in James's vision, arises from the fundamental fact of his personal history. He was born a descendant of slaves, and the culture he inherited was that of Western civilization. In the history of blacks in the world he discovered the optimism of revolt.

At the end, he claimed that his greatest contribution was to clarify and extend the heritage of Marx and Lenin.

The great distortion of the twentieth century was the perversion of Marx's essentially humanist and egalitarian approach into the totalitarianism of the Soviet empire. James was the only political thinker who claimed the heritage of Marx and Lenin and advocated democratic governments through the unfettered common sense of the general populace. It was this belief that led him to see the United States as the obvious crucible for the real birth in the future of a Marxist or socialist society. In a speech on the significance of Solidarity in Poland, delivered in 1981, he predicted the change in South Africa and then proceeded to his conviction that the United States would also generate such a movement:

> I don't know that I will see that. I have been in the world a long time. But I expect to see it in South Africa before I go and when it comes in the United States, I may be away but you can be certain that if I am away I will do my best to come back. I will have plenty to tell you but you will have plenty more to tell me about American Solidarity.[4]

His politics were never divorced from the activity of civilization, be it highbrow music and literature or popular culture. James claimed the right to an intellectual ancestry that went back to the ancient Greeks. He was staking a claim to this culture and spent his life making a critical and creative contribution to its intellectual traditions and its literature.

In so doing he was telling blacks in the West that they were doomed to accept being a minority in a white world. They were not

Africans in Africa, not Indians in India, not Chinese in China. The history of the modern world had brought them, for good or for ill, to the West, to the islands of the Caribbean, to the mainland of the United States, to Britain and Europe, and there they must stay. Their destiny is part of this whole and no other.

C.L.R. James died in his sleep of a bronchial infection in his Brixton flat on 31 May 1989. His grand nephew Darcus Howe took his body back to Trinidad as he had requested. He had also specified that the Oilfield Workers Trade Union be given charge of the final rites and that no religious mumbo-jumbo be interposed between him and his grave.

It was raining when they buried him in Tunapuna cemetery. There were a thousand tributes from writers, politicians, friends and from the calypsonians Mighty Sparrow and David Rudder. The steel bands played the 'International' and Stravinsky's *The Rite of Spring*.

NOTES

1 • ENGLAND EXPECTS

1 Letter to Constance Webb, *Special Delivery: The Letters of C.L.R. James to Constance Webb,* Ed. Anna Grimshaw, Blackwell, 1996

2 *Beyond a Boundary,* C.L.R. James, Hutchinson, 1963, p. 14

3 Ibid., p. 35

4 Ibid., p. 29

5 'The Training of an Intellectual, the Making of a Marxist' by Richard Small in *C.L.R. James: His Life and Work,* Ed. Paul Buhle, Allison and Busby, 1986

2 • THE COLONIAL PREPARES

1 Journal of Commonwealth Literature, No. 7, July 1969

2 'Discovering Literature in Trinidad: the 1930s' in *Spheres of Existence: Selected Writings,* C.L.R. James, Allison and Busby, 1980

3 *The Intelligence of the Negro: A Few Words with Doctor Harland,* The Beacon, Vol 1, No. 5, 1931

3 • THE EXILE ARRIVES IN THE KINGDOM

1 *Special Delivery: The Letters of C.L.R. James to Constance Webb*, Ed. Anna Grimshaw, Blackwell, 1996, p. 35
2 *Beyond a Boundary*, C.L.R. James, Hutchinson, 1963, p. 121
3 Ibid., p. 121
4 *Special Delivery*, p. 51
5 *An Occupation for Gentlemen*, Fredric Warburg, Hutchinson, 1959
6 Ibid. p. 214
7 *Spheres of Existence: Selected Writings*, C.L.R. James, Allison and Busby, 1980, p. 238

4 • CALL ME JOHNSON

1 Letter to Constance Webb, *Special Delivery: The Letters of C.L.R. James to Constance Webb*, Ed. Anna Grimshaw, Blackwell, 1996, p. 38
2 Ibid, p. 62.
3 Ibid, p. 66–67
4 Ibid., p. 64
5 Workers Party Pamphlet, June 1940
6 *American Civilization*, Ed. Anna Grimshaw and Keith Hart, Blackwell, 1993
7 'The Struggle for Happiness' in *American Civilization*
8 *C.L.R. James: A Critical Introduction*, Aldon Lynn Nielsen, University Press of Mississippi, 1993

5 • THROUGH THE LOOKING GLASS

1 'C.L.R. James: The Speaker and his Charisma' by Constance Webb in *C.L.R. James: His Life and Work*, Ed. Paul Buhle, Allison and Busby, 1986
2 *Special Delivery: The Letters of C.L.R. James to Constance Webb*, Ed. Anna Grimshaw, Blackwell, 1996.

6 • A BIG WHITE WHALE

1 *Mariners, Renegades and Castaways: The Story of Herman Melville and the World We Live In,* C.L.R. James, Bewick, 1978

7 • OUT OF JOINT

1 Letter to Frank Kermode, 15 September 1978

8 • HOME ALONE

1 'Every Cook Can Govern: a Study of Democracy in Ancient Greece and Negro Americans and American Politics', Correspondence Publishing Co, June 1956

9 • NO ONE COMES TO HIS PARTY

1 First published as 'Parties, Politics and Economics in the Caribbean', reprinted in *Spheres of Existence: Selected Writings,* C.L.R. James, Allison and Busby, 1980

II • WHO IS LEBRUN?

1 'Wilson Harris', 1965, in *Spheres of Existence: Selected Writings,* C.L.R. James, Allison and Busby, 1980

I2 • A STRAIGHT BAT

1 *Beyond a Boundary,* C.L.R. James, Hutchinson, 1963, p. 151
2 *Natives of My Person,* George Lamming, Holt, Rinehart and Winston, 1972

I3 • AN AFRICA OF THE MIND

1 'The Rise and Fall of Nkrumah' in *At the Rendezvous of Victory,* C.L.R. James, Allison and Busby, 1984

2 *Nkrumah and the Ghana Revolution,* C.L.R. James, Allison and
   Busby, 1977
3 Ibid., p. 12

16 • BLACK POWER AND AFTER

1 *Spheres of Existence: Selected Writings,* C.L.R. James, Allison
   and Busby, 1980, p. 229
2 Letter to Martin Glaberman, Oct 1963 reprinted in *C.L.R.
   James: His Life and Work,* Ed. Paul Buhle, Allison and Busby,
   1986, p. 159
3 *At the Rendezvous of Victory,* C.L.R. James, Allison and Busby,
   1984, p. 186
4 Ibid., p. 272–3

INDEX